Making Love with the Divine:
Sacred, Ecstatic and Erotic Experiences

Kay Louise Aldred

Girl God Books

Cover Art by Arna Baartz

©2023 All Rights Reserved

ISBN: 9798361985364

www.thegirlgod.com

Girl God Books

Mentorship with Goddess: Growing Sacred Womanhood

Mentorship with Goddess is a workbook – a year-long programme – a rite of passage – especially useful for the transition into autonomous adulthood – and also for the menopause journey. The programme can be undertaken solo or as a group. The specific aim is growing Sacred Womanhood. Mentorship with Goddess is an embodied education and evolution, which combines metacognition, intuition, and instinct. It is principally about discovering, accepting, and loving yourself, and simultaneously protecting and vulnerably showing up as your whole Self in the world.

Rainbow Goddess: Celebrating Neurodiversity

Rainbow Goddess lives within the full spectrum of the human mind. There is not one way of thinking, learning, or behaving that she does not inhabit fully and sanctify. This carnival and inclusive Goddess celebrates the gifts of those whose minds exist and operate outside the box of society's 'norms' – and she trumpets the creativity, visions, and uniqueness of these humans. Rainbow Goddess protectively arcs around those who encounter the struggles of patriarchal expectation and judgement of neurodiverse women. This Girl God anthology showcases the voices and art of women as they express their experiences of neurodiversity. It is a thanksgiving for the creativity, imagination, self-awareness, super-power sensitivity, problem-solving, planning abilities, resilience, and new ways of seeing the world that these women offer.

The Crone Initiation: Women Speak on the Menopause Journey

The Crone Initiation is an anthology of women's experiences of perimenopause and menopause, and the part Goddess plays in this journey. Crone's presence in the breakdowns and breakthroughs, the disintegration and rebuilding, is expressed through words and art. Meaning is reclaimed and the power of the Elder restored.

Re-Membering with Goddess: Healing the Patriarchal Perpetuation of Trauma

Re-Membering with Goddess is an anthology of women's experiences of trauma—trauma as a result of patriarchy; trauma perpetuated by patriarchy; and how through personal healing of trauma the Goddess is re-membered, re-embodied and resurrected. As repeating loops of trauma restriction are released—in the mind, body, and nervous system—Goddess is re-embodied and rises... and the patriarchy falls.

The Girl God

A book for children young and old, celebrating the Divine Female by Trista Hendren. Magically illustrated by Elisabeth Slettnes with quotes from various faith traditions and feminist thinkers.

-

Songs of Solstice: Goddess Carols

This Songbook celebrates the cycles of Nature—Birth, Life, and Death—through the changing Seasons (the Turning of the Wheel) from Autumn's abundance, for which we give thanks, to Winter's 'Dead Time', when even the warmth of the Sun leaves us, and the world goes dark and cold. It is a celebration of both the Light and the Dark, since both are Sacred and both are needed for new Life to grow and flourish.

Just as I Am: Hymns Affirming the Divine Female

What is a Hermnal? It's the collective sigh of our ancestral Grandmothers. It's a means of drawing us closer together as Sisters. It is a compilation of songs that affirm our Sacredness, apart from Man, and assure us that we are Sovereign Beings and Creatrixes, too. And it is our Love Gift of Gratitude to Mama.

In Defiance of Oppression – The Legacy of Boudicca

An anthology that encapsulates the Spirit of the defiant warrior in a modern apathetic age. No longer will the voices of our sisters go unheard, as the ancient Goddesses return to the battlements, calling to ignite the spark within each and every one of us—to defy oppression wherever we find it and stand together in solidarity.

Warrior Queen: Answering the Call of The Morrigan

A powerful anthology about the Irish Celtic Goddess. Each contributor brings The Morrigan to life with unique stories that invite readers to partake and inspire them to pen their own. Included are essays, poems, stories, chants, rituals, and art from dozens of storytellers and artists from around the world, illustrating and recounting the many ways this powerful Goddess of war, death, and prophecy has changed their lives.

Re-visioning Medusa: from Monster to Divine Wisdom

A remarkable collection of essays, poems, and art by scholars who have researched Her, artists who have envisioned Her, and women who have known Her in their personal story. All have spoken with Her and share something of their communion in this anthology.

New Love: a reprogramming toolbox for undoing the knots

A powerful combination of emotional/spiritual techniques, art and inspiring words for women who wish to move away from patriarchal thought. *New Love* includes a mixture of compelling thoughts and suggestions for each day, along with a 'toolbox' to help you change the parts of your life you want to heal.

How to Live Well Despite Capitalist Patriarchy

This book will serve as a starting point to challenge some of our societal assumptions, in hopes of helping women become stronger and breaking their chains.

Dedication

For my husband Dan.

Thank you for the weave we create and the love we share.
Thank you for our journey of mind, body, heart, energy, and soul.
Thank you for your willingness to go deeper and deeper.

Table of Contents

Introduction..7

Map of Your Journey 10

Before You Start 11

How to Use this Book 13

Definitions 14

Month 1 19

  Theme: Divine Nervous System

Month 2 27

  Theme: The Mundane

Month 3 33

  Theme: Words

Month 4 43

  Theme: Sound

Month 5 49

  Theme: Movement

Month 6 57

  Theme: Nature

Month 7 67

  Theme: Creating

Month 8 75

  Theme: Relating

Month 9 83

  Theme: Touch

Month 10 89

  Theme: Sexual Intimacy

Month 11 97

  Theme: Self Pleasure

Month 12 109

  Theme: Mysticism

Conclusion 117

Further Exploration 118

Thank You 119

What's Next? 121

'The very word erotic comes from the Greek word eros, the personification of love in all its aspects – born of Chaos and personifying creative power and harmony. When I speak of the erotic, then, I speak of it as an assertion of the lifeforce of women; of that creative energy empowered, the knowledge and use of which we are now reclaiming in our language, our history, our dancing, our loving, our work, our lives'.

–Audre Lorde, *'Uses of the Erotic: The Erotic as Power'*

Welcome

'The world is holy. Nature is holy. The body is holy. Sexuality is holy. The imagination is holy. Divinity is immanent in nature; it is within you as well as without'.
–Margot Adler, *Drawing Down the Moon*

This book demonstrates that sacred, ecstatic, and erotic experiences are more common than we realise. It is difficult to ascertain their exact frequency, as they are rarely talked about in mainstream spiritual and religious circles, let alone day-to-day conversation. Most of us also appear to have no conscious knowledge of the historically documented, mystical and rapturous ways of experiencing the Divine – be that God, Goddess, or Spirit – which are embedded within the antiquity of spiritual paths and the world religions.

Patriarchal concealment of these occurrences was – and still is – likely motivated by the suppression of the ability of the body to commune directly with the Divine and the power of that. This is part of a bigger agenda, of course, the ongoing undermining of the Feminine.

The two primary questions this book explores are as follows. Firstly, what are the embodied experiences of women today? And secondly, what and how does the power of the erotic express through women's bodies and how might others reclaim that for themselves?

I invite you to tune in, consider and explore these questions for yourself. When you find your own answers, I then invite you to share your story and inspire others to tune in and uncover their own answers too.

In doing so we rise, restore, and reinstate the wisdom of the erotic – the potent and creative lifeforce of women.

Art by Kat Shaw

Introduction

Making Love with the Divine: Sacred, Ecstatic, and Erotic Experiences

'See that I am God. See that I am in everything. See that I do everything'.
–Julian of Norwich

Why this book and these topics?

Love Making – The Divine – Sacred – Ecstatic – Erotic – The Body

They all 'found' me. Actually, they have been present within me from my birth and have followed me around my whole life. Nagging, messaging, urging. I've been curious and I have been explorative. I've been moved by the deep knowing that many of us have an innate yearning, a deep longing for a visceral experience of the Divine, and that we keep it buried, unconscious and hidden, because we carry shame about it.

This shame was outed and became visible when I put out a call for shares as part of the research and preparatory process for this book. Replies were sparse, even when elicited from friendship, sisterhood, or spiritual groups. I repeatedly received 'arms-length', curt, responses. Many were triggered. Most were silent. There was a lot of discomfort, shock, and disgust. I suddenly felt alien, 'different' and that my intuition and instinct were skewed – that I had misjudged and got it all wrong. I rapidly moved into working through my own discomfort at the nil and negative responses of others, plus the projections of 'you're too much' and it's all 'grotesque' being layered upon me both consciously and verbally, but also energetically and unconsciously. I journeyed deeper into my mind, heart and body asking my inner wisdom, 'what are these reactions all about? what is underneath it? what is hidden? what am I not seeing?'

The answers came through rapidly – loud and clear.

We are collectively dissociated, disconnected from our bodies. We live from and as mind – primarily functioning from cognition – cut off from our bodies. This is a deeply entrenched phenomenon in religious and spiritual communities. We still carry shame and guilt about body pleasure of any type and hold the belief that it is wicked and separates us from 'God' and access to 'heaven'. We are still carrying the conditioning that the body is sinful, evil, and cannot be trusted. We are still looking to be saved by a male God who is out there and above. We often only trust mental images, constructs, and teachings, believing we need to be told what the Divine is. We do not affirm accessing 'knowledge' of the Divine through our bodies, and neither do we accept our own personal, direct experience and gnosis as valid or truth.

We still believe the erotic is simply 'dirty sex'. We carry, in our bodies, a shame around sex, sexual pleasure and self-touch. These, and the concept of ecstasy, activate a fear and disgust response in the body. We are absolutely indoctrinated by religion and believe religious texts, clergy and tradition are the only authority about the Divine. We believe the sacred and everyday are not one in and the same. We see no divinity in or through or of the body and pleasure.

The body – particularly the body of woman – remains firmly in the grip of the Patriarchy. We continue to be controlled. Our bodies remain tamed and ensnared in the narrative of The Fall.

These revelations left me shocked, horrified, and then absolutely determined that this book needed to be written – to set us, our bodies and the Divine free.

The book originally started out as a platform for showcasing and giving language to the mystical experiences of modern-day women – which are happening all of the time –- narrating their accounts of communion with the Divine and sense of the numinous. However, it morphed and changed during the research process. Whilst these accounts remain as the backbone of the book, the format has evolved into a workbook. The storytelling of the (often unbeknown to them) contemporary mystics I interviewed and received shares from prompted me to write from a more educational lens. So, I formulated practises which I could offer to readers, within the text, with the intention of supporting them to begin the journey of liberating their body and forging their own direct pathway and access to the Divine. The book metamorphosised into a practical guide.

I am passionate about 'tangible divinity'. I write and teach about the fusion of the mundane and sacred, and the holiness of flesh. I support the remembrance that divinity is our birth right, our natural state, and that we are spiritual soma – a sacred human – fully human and fully divine.

Making love with the Divine is making love with life – allowing life to move and express through us. It is embodying creative flow, following instinct and impulse, and body messages. Making love with the Divine is aliveness. Reclaiming our sacred self, the sacredness of the mundane and ordinary, is a process through which we can access peace, contentment and meaning. In experiencing the ecstatic and erotic we are able to create with joy and are energised. Love flows. Love is made. Love is shared. This book demonstrates this is all on offer to us moment-to-moment, in day-to-day situations and life.

I am so grateful to the women who participated in the research process and shared their life experiences and inner wisdom with me. The demographic of the participants was vast, the women were from a wide range of ages, background and lived around the globe. Some shared voice notes, other emails, some sent art and poems, and others generously offered a more formal virtual interview. The process of collecting women's wisdom was humbling, profoundly impactful and a true honour. Without their grace and willingness to share so freely this book could not have been written.

The vision for the book was to anonymise the research, writing about what was shared, alongside my own first-hand experiences, which are included in each section. This was partly for the women's comfort, especially those who were sharing deeply intimate information. The main reason, however, was so that contributors spoke 'as one'. They spoke as 'woman' – a unified voice and body. Women's bodies are programmed to make love with the Divine fluidly and organically. It is our birth right to live pleasurably and commune with the sacred within the mundane. In keeping shares anonymous, the aim is that any reader can imagine herself in the experience. It is of her body.

Once the window of sharing closed, I knew it was time to collate and process 'woman's voice'. All shares were anonymised and woven into the text alongside research and my own gnosis, thematically and anecdotally so we became one. We speak as one. The voice moves from I – to we and mine – to ours. Individual to collective and shared experience. Woman. The Feminine. She. Making Love with the Divine. I surrendered into process and flow, asking that I be guided and be of service to Life itself – and that the book catalyse Lovemaking with the Divine in all who read it. I released control knowing that none of this is about me.

One of the women I interviewed said to me 'my deepest longing is to make myself and my life a prayer'. Making Love with the Divine is just that – living in constant communication, rapport, and union with goodness.

Map of Your Journey

Before You Start

'Pleasure is a gateway to accessing your fullest, truest personhood'.
–Emily Nagoski, Come as you are: The surprising new science that will transform your sex life

How does aliveness move and express through you?

How do you make love with the divine?

How is the sacred a living aspect of your life?

There are times in our life when we feel extra-ordinarily alive. This may be a one-off, a single moment in time, when we suddenly feel totally integrated, connected to ourselves, or another, or the world. Or it may be a place, resource or activity we have incorporated into our day-to-day life, because we know it is there and during it that we move beyond the mundane and into the realm of the sacred – feel expansive, ecstatic even – and totally in flow and union – both fully ourselves and simultaneously fully connected to something that is beyond ourselves, – the erotic, a force, the Divine.

These encounters are beyond words. They are numinous and mystical. Yet, within this book I wanted to capture how contemporary women are still accessing and communing with magic through their bodies. How they are making love with the Divine in a plethora of ways. How we know through these occurrences, that there is more in this realm than just the 'common place' and that we channel lifeforce, creating with the divine through pleasure: self-pleasure, sexual union, movement, art, gardening – and as I discovered – so many other ways I hadn't even considered.

You are about to undertake a journey of self-discovery. Commit to this. Then prepare and reflect.

Start by thinking about your thinking:

- *How and what do you think about the Divine?*
- *Who taught you this?*
- *Are your ideas actually your own? If not, where do they come from?*

Then think about your understanding of the book's key words:

- *Making love*

- *Sacred*

- *Erotic*

- *Mystical*

- *Ecstatic*

- *Lifeforce*

- *Aliveness*

- *Pleasure*

How do you define them? Are the definitions your own or something you have inherited?

Next notice your body responses to the above. Is it different than your mind's response? Does your body's reaction tell you something different than your thoughts? Are there any surprises?

The journey of this book is about exploration, curiosity, and discovery. You will get out of this year what you give. All that is really needed from you is your time, commitment, and willingness to reflect, listening to your mind, body, and heart. You cannot do this wrong. You cannot get it wrong. Aliveness and pleasure will teach you; the shares in the book may resonate and awaken you more deeply to your own knowing and what you experience through all of this is your truth. That is the learning. Instead of learning through suffering we can learn through life and pleasure, lifeforce animating through us, supporting us to embody our truth.

If you wish to be in community, there is a Making Love with the Divine Private Facebook Group for those who have a copy of the book. You are welcome to join here: https://www.facebook.com/groups/makinglovewiththedivine.

There is also a forthcoming Making Love with the Divine Evergreen Online Course. Be sure you are signed up for my newsletter for updates. https://www.kaylouisealdred.com/contact.html

How to Use this Book

Having now seen a visual representation of the *Making Love with the Divine Exploratory Journey* (see Map of the Journey page) you can see that it is a year-long, month-by-month process. Each month follows the same structure and includes a:

- **Theme**

- **Discussion** (which weaves in women's wisdom and shares)

- **'Try this' section** (which has a practice for you to explore)

You will already have reflected on your thinking and made a commitment to be curious (see the *Before You Start* page). You can work through the book on your own, with a friend or in a group. Move through the book month-by-month in numerical order over a year. You can start at any time of the year. You will need time to absorb, reflect and integrate so try not to race ahead. This is a different way of discovery, understanding and experiencing divinity and life. It is self-discovery of union and gnosis – one that is led by your body and lifeforce, not your mind.

How you make love with the divine will be unique to you, most likely different than others, including your friends, so, if possible, stay away from comparison. There is nothing really 'to do' other than open to receptivity – to Life moving through you. If the theme of the month does not resonate or facilitate that flow, then leave it and tune into experiences that do. Your inner mystic may not commune with the divine the way offered in that particular month. Trust and listen to yourself.

Finally, please note that none of the information presented in this book is meant to replace the advice of a medical, health, legal and/or any other professional or service. How you choose to act on the words and content is of your own determination and free will.

Definitions

Before you read this content, ensure you have read the *Before You Start* section of the book and defined these words for yourself. Your definitions may well change as you move through the year or even immediately, after you have read this page – however it is always wise and empowering to self-reference and defer to your own responses and inner knowing first. Start where you are.

Those women who engaged in the process of longer and more in-depth sharing were asked how they understood or defined the following words and concepts which the book explores. Shares were rich and are summarised here alongside my own personal understanding, research, and wider reading in order to offer you a starting point and landscape of the book content.

Artists, writers, poets, dancers, musicians have tried to express these concepts and definitions through their art. A beautiful example of this and a personal favourite – the creative expression of love making with the Divine – is Sonnet III: Love's *Testament* by Dante Gabriel Rossetti.

What is Love Making?

For me, in the context of this book, love making is the process and production of love, love manifest. Some women described this as a sexual activity, as is the dictionary definition.

What is Love?

This feels like an important question to examine as the book is addressing lovemaking with the Divine. Thinking about what is actually being made seemed a sensible point to consider. Love was described as affection, attraction, warmth, trust, and benevolence. Love can be defined as a frequency, and energy which flows from us outward, as well as an energy which is activated in relationship. Yet the participant shares about how they make love with the Divine were far deeper and broader. Although all the types of love listed below were alluded to, no one used these exact terms. There was a direct correlation in the way lovemaking with the Divine was described by the participants and the eight types of love defined by the Ancient Greeks:

1. Eros (sexual passion)
2. Philia (deep friendship)
3. Ludus (playful love)
4. Agape (love for everyone)
5. Pragma (longstanding love)
6. Philautia (love of the self)
7. Storge (family love)

8. Mania (obsessive love)

What is The Divine?

I can summarise how participants defined the Divine as everything and nothing and as a non-gendered totality of divine masculine and divine feminine, the One. One participant described the Divine as 'spirit' and both male and female, and yet neither. Another described the Divine as 'Love from which we come and return to when we leave this body – it is God/Goddess, all that is'. Most women found it hard to put their thoughts and feelings into words and described the Divine as an energy, value, quality, or thing. Descriptions included 'source energy that is everywhere and in me – that unites all', 'feminine and masculine energy balanced', 'beyond words', the 'substance which glues us all together – wise, honest and complete' and 'loving presence – we can't see but can feel'. Only one participant chose to use the word 'God' but qualified her choice explaining that by 'God' she meant – 'genderless energy, oneness that doesn't give a flying fuck if we are good or bad'. She went on saying 'we are the God particle – we just need to remember and light up with it'. I loved this!

What does it mean to make love with the Divine?

Answers to this question were mostly a description of union and the process of two becoming one and birthing love. Most saw this as a process of being united together with someone or something. One contributor described this as a 'healing of splits' – the schism of the spiritual, physical, mental, and emotional. Another talked about this in a comparable way, as a 'bridging' and another as 'joyous connection'. Other descriptions included 'full presence and conscious awareness', 'ultimate connection' and 'appreciation, the sudden I am'.

It seems to also, for most women, it includes the experience of relinquishing control and a letting 'yourself be loved', –Rev Rowan Bombadil, *Igniting Intimacy: Sex magic rituals for practical living and loving.*

What is an experience?

Experiences are events or happenings which leave an impact on a person. In this book the focus is on embodied, lived experiences of contemporary, 'ordinary' and secular women. The women interviewed were not in religious orders, they were not nuns or ordained priests.

What is meant by Sacred?

Women expressed, on the whole, that this word was associated with the Divine and holiness and signifying something to be respected. Most also declared the sacred to be a personal, physical, and concrete experience. It was described as the 'preciousness of the personal – my subjective connection with the Divine' and also 'anything our heart calls us to'. One woman expressed that 'it feels pure, magical, universal and very loving and I feel a deep, deep reverence, I realise how natural sacred is, from the earth and universe'. Another participant explained that the sacred was an 'embodied, physical or dense form of the divine' – 'things are sacred – sacred body, sacred ritual object'. Finally, women defined the sacred as 'each and every thing' and a state of 'being here connected' and with 'the intention to make anything more of a prayer' through 'connection and conversation with the Divine'. 'It's the opposite to 'productivity mode' one woman said.

What is meant by Erotic?

As humans we are born to create. We have an instinct to create, and a need to birth. This is a primal urge. This creative principle, the desire to reproduce 'life', is eros. Freud talked about it in terms of life instinct and the energy of libido – sexual coupling, birthing humans, preserving the survival of humanity – and that it was the polemic of thanatos, the death instinct – an aggressive energy – self destructive behaviour.

In its primal energetic sense, recovered from patriarchal binding, the erotic is not sexualised but instead is the innocent, childlike, 'felt sense of aliveness', the pure, raw, unconditioned energy of wonderment, awe, and curiosity. As quoted at the start if the book, Audre Lorde wrote in *Uses of the Erotic: The Erotic as Power* that 'the very word erotic comes from the Greek word eros, the personification of love in all its aspects – born of chaos and personifying creative power and harmony. When I speak of the erotic, then, I speak of it as an assertion of the lifeforce of women; of that creative energy empowered, the knowledge and use of which we are now reclaiming in our language, our history, our dancing, our loving, our work, our lives'.

Women who contributed shares to this book had startlingly different definitions for this word and many were wary of what it represented. Some intrinsically felt it was linked to sexual energy and 'arousal', the 'physical tapping into sacred sexual connection'. One participant shared her vulnerability, stating that although to her it 'doesn't necessarily have anything to do with sexual pleasure, I shy away from this word and the feelings it arouses, but I also know I have a very, very, deep pent up erotic energy somewhere in my lower belly, and sometimes I feel she might burst out and scream and roar like a lion'.

The power of the erotic and its presence within the body was palpable in women's voices. It 'looks and feels like powerful spirals of pulsing energy' one said. It is the 'blood red lifeforce from Mother Earth, traversing through all of my chakras' said another. The erotic was described as the 'energy of lifeforce', 'kundalini energy', 'that which makes us spirit' and 'love'. Finally, the erotic was expressed as a doorway to 'pleasure, expansion' and the Divine, an 'opening to receive and commune'.

What is meant by Ecstatic?

The ecstatic is beyond the self, the I, the human animal aspect of us. It involves an effable mystical encounter – awe-filled, mysterious, metaphysical, paradoxically within the physical body. The ecstatic is the portal of the experience of our full humanity, simultaneously with our full divinity. It is an experience which goes beyond pleasure and is the convergence of 'emotion, intuition, mysticism and sex', –Barbara Carrellas, *Ecstasy is Necessary: A Practical Guide*.

It was described as 'a place of bliss – for example sexual lovemaking or looking at a sunrise' and a 'full somatic experience of dancing with the Divine'. One participant described it as 'the interdimensional inside of us turned on' which is 'always accessible if I drop my resistance to feeling it'.

There was a wariness of the ecstatic. 'I'm still working on this level of feeling' said one woman and another expressed that the ecstatic was 'cathartic' and a 'searching for presence' that 'lacks integration'.

Art by Arna Baartz

Art by Arna Baartz

Month 1
Theme: Divine Nervous System

'Be still and know that I am God'.
—Psalm 46:10

'Who is She? She is your power, your Feminine source. Big Mama. The Goddess. The Great Mystery. The web-weaver. The life force. The first time, the twentieth time you may not recognize her. Or pretend not to hear. As she fills your body with ripples of terror and delight'.
—Lucy H. Pearce, *Burning Woman*

Discussion:

'Be still' – engage the parasympathetic nervous system – *'and know'* – internally, through your embodied felt sense – *'that I am'* – that the truth of who you are – *'God'* – is Divine.

What if the Divine is actually the resolution of trauma and the flow of a regulated nervous system?

What if making love with the Divine is living as fully human and fully divine, moving in and out of activation and deactivation, sympathetic and parasympathetic, nervous system states?

Many of us have travelled a long way on our spiritual path. We have journeyed up and down, above and below, outside, and then finally, very firmly back inside our bodies. As seekers, and in many ways a doubting Thomas(ina)s, we have needed to feel, see, touch, smell and hear the Divine to genuinely believe in it. As embodied mystics, the more contact we make with embodied sacred states, the more we move toward our physiology and start to 'merge' spirit and merge at an ever-deeper level within mind, body, and heart.

There comes a time when we recognise that mindfulness, meditation, prayer, and even breathwork and yoga, are supportive blissful experiences but mainly in a dissociated and disembodied way. We finish our practices and feel disconnected, going about our day-to-day embodied, human life. We start to no longer feel satisfied with 'being' with the Divine in a fragmented and unintegrated way.

Energy medicine training introduced me to the concept of cosmic and earthly energetics moving through the body and I started to make connections with electromagnetic fields, basic physics, and religious and spiritual concepts. Angels became rays of the rainbow light spectrum; eros became the pulsating energy of the earth; and the Divine became magnetic and electric forces. I liked the harmonising of different disciplines and paths coming together, uniting and complementing each other. I liked there not having to be either this way or that way. It felt good in my body and my mind.

Over the last couple of years, understanding and working with trauma and its resolution, somatics, and nervous system regulation, has brought me into expansive states of embodied flow and wellness. A sudden expansion of perception, working in accordance with my embodied knowing, resulted in a comprehension and felt sense of the imminence of the Divine. Goddess-God and the ideals I had sought, such as peace, clarity, connection, love, and holy anger, were the internal experiences of a regulated nervous system. Living as a Divine Human, the embodiment of Goddess-God and as the 'I am', for me, is being within a body which activates and moves through its day with regulated sympathetic activation, and which comes regularly into rest and communion in the parasympathetic state.

My discovery is that all I seek and 'petition' the Divine for, including oneness, acceptance, gratitude, protection, safety companionship and belonging, are natural states of nervous system health and trauma resolution. Through nervous system regulation I am making love with the Divine.

I am not a nervous system specialist. What I do know, through embodied experience, is that I have experienced deeply sacred, erotic, and ecstatic experiences within a variety of nervous system states. As I explain below the Divine is within sympathetic activation, the get up and go state as well as within parasympathetic deactivation, the rest and digest state. The Divine inhabits, with ease, the rhythmic and cyclical flow of regulation, the ebb and flow of my breathing and the rise and fall of my chest. I make love with the Divine through my mammalian animal form and its physiological functions.

I breathe in, come into the felt-sense of readiness for action – sharp, precise, strong, stable, protective – what some may call my 'masculine energy' – aspect of God state. I breathe out, coming into the felt sense of beingness – releasing, resting, nurturing, wisdom, receiving – what some may call my 'feminine energy' – aspect of Goddess state. I breathe in, feeling expansion, sacred rage, protection of the innocence, activism ignited – my warrioress state – aspect of Goddess. I breathe out, feeling contained, sacred guardianship, the path, logical structure clarified – my warrior state – aspect of God.

And so, this enquiry goes on as I track my nervous system and the symbiosis of mind, body, energy – weaving. Soon it all becomes non-gendered and an ecstatic symphony. There are no boundaries or classifications, no labels, rules or spiritual practices, no teachers, gurus, or books – it all becomes a flowing stream of 'isness' of lifeforce (the erotic perhaps) flowing through me, which I observe, feel, and experience. And in this being alive, an incarnated human, deeply embodied and ecstatic, simultaneously within a sacred and mundane process, I am making love with the Divine. Barbara Carrellas writes in her book, *Ecstasy is Necessary*, 'ecstatic experience is the reason for human life on this physical plane'.

Being able to hold space – be with the full spectrum of my body's sensations and nervous system processes – has brought me into relation with the extraordinary ecstatic experience of embodiment. Instinct and intuition are truly sacred. I deeply feel the divinity and sacredness of the inhale and exhale, expansion, and contraction, activating the loving making of the double helix activation of my DNA and the electrical erotic spark and flow within my central nervous system – creating life. My nervous system regulation and action is deeply erotic and mystical – a profound mystery of electric sparks, energy and powerhouse of all sensation and symbiotic experience (physical, energetic, and spiritual). As Marion Woodman and Elinor Dickson write in *Dancing in the Flames, The Dark Goddess in the Transformation of Consciousness*, 'As we begin to look at the quantum reality of nature and of our own bodies, we are called to a new level of consciousness. In many ways, we are discovering what we have intuitively known for centuries. In psychological terms this is the yin/yang reality, separate but indivisible. While the new metaphors – 'chaos theory', 'quantity reality' – speak more directly to contemporary culture, the ancient yin/yang and Shakti/ Shiva realities still hold true'.

The numinous is something I personally connect with through my body, most especially, my nervous system. *What is the numinous?* Definitions include (www.merriam-webster.com/dictionary/numinous):

Supernatural and mysterious

Filled with a sense of the presence of divinity

Appealing to the higher emotions or to the aesthetic sense

I inhale deeply and feel activation, excitement, faster heartbeat, my rapid breath, and joy as my rib cage expands, meeting a friend's new-born baby for the first time, my nervous system expressing a felt sense of the mystery. I hold the baby in my arms and breathe out the erotic wonderment of this innocent being, knowing in this connective moment that there is nothing beyond the miracle of safe relationship.

I return home and read about another sexual assault online, and I sympathetically activate in my nervous system again, this time in anger, expressing a low growl, loud and powerful exhale, opening the uterus, feeling the erotic and sacred power of the earth's volcanic energy, and the presence of the Dark Goddesses within me.

I take extra time in bed on the following weekend morning, watching the fractals of light from early morning sunshine dancing on the ceiling and I sink into the mattress and warmth of the duvet even more deeply, in a parasympathetic, sacred state of oneness with all of life, connected and held. Half an hour later, I feel the hand of my partner move onto my sacrum, his touch electrifies and activates my sympathetic nervous system, arousal, and my skin and his hand ecstatically make divine love through that instantaneous touch.

The Divine Nervous System, our extra sensory perception, is an embodied process in which the unity of animal and spirit is evidenced, human and divine, within our flesh as we experience through its regulatory movement the sacred, erotic, and ecstatic. The haven – the still small voice – is in the centre of making love with the Divine, in stillness and nervous system regulation. Love making with the Divine starts within us, relating to ourselves internally in our body – we then take the love made and make love with the Divine externally, in our relating and exchanging.

Making love with the Divine through and within the Divine Nervous system is flowing with the oscillating waves of parasympathetic and sympathetic surges – staying present and connected to ourselves – our body, sensation, mind, and thoughts – whilst simultaneously staying connected to environment and others without being lost or distracted within any one aspect of this. To make love with the Divine is to be one with the entirety of life – 'the same lifeforce energy that flows through us also flows through every living thing on the planet; we are in an ongoing erotic relationship with all of life, all of the time. How much of it we see, feel, or appreciate is dependent upon how much if this energy we have learned to recognise, accept, and allow'. –Barbara Carrellas, *Ecstasy is Necessary: A Practical Guide*

Although all participants in the research (bar one) did not directly talk about the nervous system, many talked about their experiences of making love with the Divine in a tantric sense – a weaving together of physical and spiritual – and alluded to the energy and experience of balance. One woman talked about making love with the Divine as a raising of kundalini, which lies latent and coiled at the base of the spine and once activated moves up the highway of the spine and nervous system. She said that through this, the Divine 'abides within us' and 'makes us spirit' so there is 'no distinction' and the divine and us are 'just one'. This love making with the Divine in her view is 'limitless', 'blissful', and embodied – 'every single part is relaxed and open'.

Her detailed description of 'sacred union; and 'two sides coming together at a zero point' – where there is a 'transitory' 'divine explosion of heart and mind' – echoed the nervous system regulatory flow of deactivation and rest, activation and doing. This participant also expressed that she felt making love with the Divine happens 'everywhere and in everything' and at 'an atomic level' – it being an internal physiological mystical and ecstatic process within our sacred flesh.

Another participant talked in detail of embodied erotic union and making love to the Divine also through raising kundalini within her, and up through the nervous system through spiralling her body, moving the energy to 'awaken spine energy'. She expressed this was an organic process with 'no thought' and was a 'physical movement of the body'.

A final contributor talked about embodied erotic union and making love with the Divine as 'presence', 'being with myself', 'my skin' and 'my senses' and 'listening to what comes'. She expressed that although she had experienced highly charged, sympathetic nervous system states – and peak and cathartic experiences through activities such as 'ecstatic dance' – she was always tired 'after the peak' and so was now 'slowing down and looking for a distinct experience' of the Divine, within the engagement of the parasympathetic nervous system. She expressed that she felt the types of highly charged sympathetic ecstatic experiences she had gone through 'lacked integration' and a longer-term lovemaking with the Divine. She was looking for the middle ground, lovemaking with the Divine through a more regulatory nervous system state.

Art by Arna Baartz

Try this: Hands of light practice

Do this practice two or three times a week during the month.

This practice is designed to support you in exploring your whole self in a sacred and gentle way, and tune into your nervous system – offering you a moment's pause, a moment to be still and know yourself as fully human and fully divine. It facilitates embodied divine union, a tantric experience and exploration of self-awareness. In addition, it is highly regulatory for your nervous system and so has wellbeing benefits for you mentally, physically, energetically, emotionally, and spiritually. It enhances your intuition and instinct and awareness of how your body is constantly lovemaking with the Divine. Most of all it offers you an experience of erotic innocent presence with all that is.

Preparation:

You need to find a quiet space where you can sit and be warm, comfortable and will be undisturbed for 20 minutes.

The Practice:

As you enter the room, pause and notice its size, shape, temperature, colour, smell, lighting. Pay attention to your body's reaction. Is it happy to be in this space for 20 minutes?

If you are happy to proceed sit down.

Take a moment to feel your feet on the ground. Your bottom on the chair, the support of your back. Feel where you end and the chair starts, where your feet end, and the floor starts. Orient yourself to the room. Look around at the objects, walls, floor, and ceiling. Scan the whole room. Allow your eyes to rest on anything which captures interest.

Then gently clasp your hands together. The aim is not a grip, instead a gentle loving clasp. Pause and feel the contact of skin-on-kin. The temperature, smoothness or otherwise any other sensations.

Drop your shoulders and breathe. Don't force anything.

You can look at your hands as they touch or simply feel them whilst looking around the room.

Continue exploring the hand this way for 2–3 minutes.

Then pause. Feel your feet on the floor, bottom on the chair and back against the chair.

This time, bring the hands together without touching and imagine a ball of light between them. Notice how the ball of light is forming from a stream of energy flowing from the centre of the palms. Explore this – feeling, observing, looking, moving the hands.

When you feel a ball of light has fully formed hold it in only one hand, releasing the other onto your lap.

Pause.

Feel the ball in your hand, feet on the floor, bottom on the chair, back against the chair.

Then scan your body. Is there an area of your body calling for your presence? If so, does it want to be touched? Held? Soothed? Listened to? Witnessed?

Take the ball of light to it. Imagine the ball of light absorbing into the skin as your hand gently and reverently contacts your body.

Pause. Feel your hand's contact with your skin/clothes/body area. Make the touch sacred, reverent, worshipful, loving. Feel your feet on the floor, bottom on the chair, back against the chair.

Then LISTEN. Keep breathing – keep in the nervous system regulatory flow with the inhale and exhale, the rise and fall of the chest. And LISTEN.

L Listen
Listen and learn. Stay present to what arises in body, sensation, emotions, mind, and thoughts.
I Include
Include and compassionately allow everything that you experience.
G Greet
Greet and welcome all you experience as lovemaking with the Divine.
H Hear
Hear and receive messages and guidance.
T Thank
Thank your body, mind, emotions, and energy for coming into union.

Stay with your hand of light on that body area for as long as needed. You can move the hand to another area if you would like to.

Art by Arna Baartz

Month 2
Theme: The Mundane

'I am an expression of the divine, just like a peach is, just like a fish is'.
–Alice Walker, *The Colour Purple*

Discussion:

The mundane – our humdrum, monotonous, repetitive, run-of-the-mill, secular, temporal, day-to-day existence. Can we make love with the Divine within it? According to many participants in the research for this book the answer is most definitely yes! In fact, it is within the earthly and non-spiritual that women experienced their deepest and most profound experiences of the erotic and its aliveness. Responses included 'pausing and sitting in nature', 'walking the dog', 'playing a joke', 'laughing', 'morning run in the sunshine', 'chopping vegetables' and 'watching fish or birds'.

As Jung wrote, 'everything the anima' (soul) 'touches becomes numinous' (Carl Jung, *CW 9i, para 59*). So, embracing everything as sacred – with reverence, as divine – allows us to make love with the Divine moment-to-moment, even in the dull and wearisome tedium of regular routine. Everything can be erotic.

Tantra (which has its origins in Hindu and Buddhist philosophy) teaches that all elements, even the most unremarkable of the secular, carnal and material realm have an unquenchable, endless, Divine feminine power woven within it. Hindus name this as Shakti, the divine feminine principle, which powers up and creates all life. Barbara Carrellas writes in *Urban Tantra: Sacred Sex for the Twenty-First Century*, 'Tantra teaches us that by embracing everything in life and delving into it totally, anything can be turned into transformative, ultimately ecstatic, experience'.

Making love with the Divine is a fully embodied, grounded, earthy experience.

My own experience of this is usually multi-sensory. The ecstasy of hanging freshly washed white bedlinens on the line is potent, even more so is the process of collecting it off the line at the end of a warm and windy day. Feeling the warmth of the cotton and the unique smell of sun parched cotton is deeply erotic. Making the bed with these clean sheets, having a warm bath, and then getting into the bed and feeling my warm, soft, plump, silky skin against the crisp cotton, inhaling the scent of the sun-filled windy air still lingering on the sheets is a love making, highly charged, erotic and ecstatic experience for me. The Divine presence is there throughout the entire day within the mundane bed changing process. The feminine energy creates a multi-sensory union of the elements, cotton, and my skin, which offers me a sense of the numinous – the mystery of the expansion of this mundane 'task' into a deeply sacred experience through which aliveness dances. Pausing, breathing, calling in the senses to deeply treasure and amplify the pleasure of each step builds the ecstatic bliss. There is more going on than my limbs and a bedsheet interacting. There is an aliveness, the Divine, making love with me through it.

I recall that I was even more connected to the sacredness of the mundane in childhood. I have the strongest memories of feeling oneness and aliveness, being connected to that which was beyond just myself in the most mundane experiences. Bare feet on the coal fire ash my grandfather used to create paths in his allotment – the burning smell, the crunch sounds, the black charred coal remnants a stark contrast to the rich, fertile earth and green shoots. Standing on a stool, feeling dizzy as I balanced and reached into a mixing bowl, feeling and smelling the rich, yeasty aroma of fresh dough I was kneading to make 'stottie loaves' with my grandmother. Sitting by the coal fire on the threadbare, singed carpet; my face burning, watching the dough rise, intoxicated on the scent, salivating, waiting. Tasting the first freshly torn piece of the warm bread, salty butter dripping, running down my tiny hands, hot and silky. Licking my fingers, sucking the fat from them.

These sacred, ritualistic yet mundane, 'ordinary', embodied experiences are imprinted on my mind, heart, body as innocently erotic, when the Divine love flowed and ecstatically amplified the day to day.

One of the most profound ecstatic and erotic moments of my childhood was when I was outside in the back yard standing barefoot in cold running water, flowing from the tap my mother was filling her watering can with. I can remember sensing the sacredness of the water, feeling boundaries between my flesh and the element dissolve and the moment of shapeshifting into the element. Looking at the diamond droplets merge as my own skin transformed into light and fluidity. Closing my eyes, I held up my arms to the sun, feeling it beat down on the palms of my hands and enter into my bones. I felt the alchemy of fire and water within every cell in my body and in the instance saw in my mind's eye every creature of the sea and sky within me. I felt myself flowing in oceans, jumping across volcanos, soaring through the sky at the level of the highest bird I had ever seen at that time, a seagull. I was a channel of oneness, all life, through my body. My body was diamond rays of light – I was vibrating, humming, the freezing coldness of the water on my feet uniting with the powerful heat of the sun pulsating through my palms. I was water and fire, burning ice and submerged elevation. I was absolutely everything – ecstatic, erotic, sacred union – making love with the Divine – standing in a mundane, grounded, temporal moment of a stream of running tap water in my backyard, one summer's day, aged around 7 or 8 years.

Erotic innocence is the human birthright to live in a naturally erotic and ecstatic state – a constant embodied union with the Divine and an awe-filled, curious, spontaneous existence of oneness with the natural world through the five senses of touch, smell, sight, taste, and hearing. Children naturally inhabit this, and we have a lot to learn from them. They live magically and pleasurably when free, safe, and unrestrained. They play with and fully process their food – squishing, holding, throwing, spitting. They are in full embodied union with it. They take their time – they fully breathe in and out. They never rush. They trust their bodies, they please their bodies, bodies lead the way and interactions. For children, the mundane is sacred – everything is alive and to be discovered. There is wonderment as flesh and spirit are one – the analytical mind, not yet online – all aspects of life are one big mystical adventure.

I recalled, when preparing this chapter of the book, the first time I pulled a carrot from the ground in my grandfather's allotment. I was small enough to be crouching and be at eye level with the carrot top. I remember wondering if the carrot would hurt if I pulled it. I remember asking permission, 'is it ok carrot if I pull you up?' and feeling yes. I pulled it – absolutely ecstatic to see the orange appear from the dark earth. I remember lovingly brushing off the earth from the carrot – checking that it was ok. I danced the carrot on the ground and my hand, singing a sacred carrot song of gratitude. I smelled it. I knew my tummy wanted it. I waited. I thanked it and then knew it was ok to eat it. I sucked the end. Tasting the juice. Life poured into my stomach – aliveness, lifeforce. It was an erotic moment. And then I crunched and made noises of satisfaction – umm, yummy and felt totally unified with the earth and her abundance. I was vibrating, shimmering, full of eros, Gaia's energy. I had made love with the Divine.

Many women recalled experiences with nature and gardening whilst contributing to research for this book which I will address later. Many talked about bringing presence and consciousness to mundane activity in order to make love with the Divine when child rearing, preparing family meals and even doing the school run. These 'dull' experiences were consciously made sacred through intention, which will be further explored in later months.

In gratitude and appreciation, one woman said that she had chosen to live this earthly life in a 'love bubble'. This choice, she believed, was the transformative ingredient which alchemised her life experience and day-to-day mundane tasks, into sacred, erotic, and ecstatic living.

One of the most profound shares on the relationship of the mundane and making love with the Divine was one participant's description of how she makes the ritual of preparing a cup of coffee erotic. I'm sure that those of us who love coffee will relate to this. Even if you do not substitute the description and process for preparing your favourite drink. This participant described how she was also intentionally planning pauses into her daily schedule, consciously bringing herself into the present, the 'being here' now – taking a moment to listen to 'what is coming up'. Her daily cup of coffee appeared to have become an inertially sacred ritual (more about these later) – where she consciously creates an ecstatic moment, calling in her full aliveness and channelling the erotic.

After listening to her description my whole body was on alert, excited, longing. I was salivating and deeply desired a cup of coffee. 'Everything can be erotic' she said, even 'making a cup of coffee'. Creating space to be, time for self, to breathe. 'Simple things can be erotic and nonsexual'. She paused and exhaled. Her body dropped, she changed gear, her tone was languid. I imagined her calling in the sacred, the bliss of life, reverently choosing her favourite cup, her body and nervous system activating in anticipation of bliss and joy. I am 'making coffee', feeling the heat of the water, the steam, pouring it over the freshly ground beans, inhaling the rich, unique, sensuous 'smell', seeing the rich, distinct, earthy 'colour of the liquid'. Savouring – making love to the Divine, the earth's creation, feeling alive, longing, connected, embodied.

Coffee preparing and consuming was an expression of the Divine, just like the peach and fish.

Try this: Making love with the ordinary

This practice is about cultivating embodied mindfulness to expand your experience of the ordinary to the extra-ordinary, so you experience more aliveness in the moment and ecstatic and erotic Divine presence, making love through the mundane.

Part 1: Think of a day-to-day activity you do which brings you some pleasure or a moment's pause already. This could be a morning shower, an evening bath or making a cup of tea or coffee.

For the first two weeks of this month, set the intention to amplify this and fully engage your five senses each time you do it. So, before you begin the activity, pause, and consciously decide to make the activity sacred, to be a process of union with you and the Divine. Try and increase the time you spend on the activity noticing what you smell, taste, see, hear, and feel. As you notice, stay connected to the ground, your pelvis, and your heart. If your mind chatters and is busy you could add a narrative silently or aloud as to what you observe.

E.g., I am turning on the shower – setting the temperature for maximum warmth and pleasure. I'm noticing how liberating it feels to remove my clothes and allow all my skin and internal organs to be free. As I step into the shower, I feel my feet connect with the warm liquid and enjoy the contrast between hot at ground level and the cooler skin of my upper torso. I'm hearing the flowing torrent of water and my stomach is knotting with excitement. Once in the shower, the pounding against my skin of the water is rattling on my back and my skin is raised in goosebumps at the pleasure of that. I smell my skin more strongly as the water bounces off it.

And so on.

You will start to sense the ecstasy and eroticism of the task as you engage a multisensory processing of it. You'll move into the tantric realms of love making with the divine in the everyday.

Part 2: Once this is embedded, expand this tantric process into more challenging activities, e.g., difficult conversations with family, traffic jams, the supermarket shop. Stay with the senses, engage the narrative. If you notice smells, sounds, feelings, visuals, tastes which are distasteful and which become harder to digest, search within the moment for the pleasure and/or notice the power of your body. This is making love with the Divine through embodied reactivity which have been labelled as negative, but which are a part of aliveness and the erotic – anger, disgust – and are part of lovemaking with the Divine – sacred messages. They are all part of what is. Aliveness as one participant states, and as I have already shared, 'doesn't give a flying fuck if you are good or bad' – instead, it opens the portal or shows us the pathway 'for wanting more'. In order to access that, we are mentored and shown through our body sensations and emotions where boundaries need to be set, which support us to move through the anger and disgust, and, as she expressed 'wake up and expand'.

Art by Arna Baartz

Month 3
Theme: Words

'You burn me…'
–Sappho (Greek poet c. 630 – c. 570 BCE)

'In the beginning was the Word'.
–John 1:1

Discussion:

During the course of the research process, I was curious if any of the participants felt they made love with the Divine through writing. Although they did not 'frame' or describe the activity like this, they certainly expressed that they were a channel through which they, as one participant expressed, 'talk and connect'. Journaling for several women was a sacred undertaking, a ritual during which they consciously tapped into an aspect of themselves which was 'spiritual', 'soul', 'wise'. They expressed that they approached their time journaling with reverence and as an open invitation to gain clarity and receive guidance. They were weaving, receiving, and making love with divine guidance.

Those women who wrote more formally, academically, and as published authors described how they become 'open' and 'a vessel'. One woman expressed that, 'I pray before I write' and become a channel. She was calling in a cocreation with the Divine and love making through her words with a source other than herself – a source of aliveness and lifeforce, eros. Another writer expressed that during the writing process she remains 'open to what needs to be said'. Notice again the importance of the opening to something, an expansion, and a tapping in. She then described that there 'is a lyricism' to the writing procedure. She appeared to listen and wait and hear the sounds and tone of her work. She said she is waiting for it to 'sound right and have the right vibration'. Her love making with the Divine through words was a sacred process, again a weaving, and she said she sometimes leaves and returns to a written piece several times until she 'knows when it is finished'. She has 'knowing' and internal guidance where the vibration, the sound of her writing, matched that of 'spirit' – the Divine moving through it.

My own practice of writing is not as tempered or as graceful as the women I interviewed. When I write, I burn. Eros, lifeforce, the desire to create, scorches me. I recognise now – with experience –that I must support my body to hold the energy and the fire of the erotic – the force of Life – as it births through me. This is a sacred experience; I have to be measured and take regular breaks. I have to simultaneously midwife, as well as labour and birth. After the moments of pause – the rest – I then invite in the Divine – Lifeforce – which I have found to be responsive to requests to turn down and up as I instruct and to be entirely respectful and consensual. We then make love. My mind, heart, womb, hand, and soul all work together, cocreating with Lifeforce through thought and writing.

If I force or block the flow of Lifeforce with my own agenda or with the ideas of others, I freeze and go blank.

When I follow impulse, flashes of thought, the urge to express on topics and words which spontaneously want to be written all gush, they literally pour out of me. This flow can easily become a torrent if the topic I am addressing is clearly aligned with my own integrity and truth – if it originates from my divinity and is resonant at a soul level. The torrent blazes through me. The stream of divine erotic words is constant in the two days before menstruation, a time when I am fully connected. The fire burns more constantly and intensely now that I am in perimenopause. Perhaps this is something to do with my physiology sensing encroaching physical death, working in tandem with eros, in a 'it's now or never' kind of way.

Writing and speaking, particularly teaching, are two primary ways I make love with the Divine. The experience is one of oxymoron and paradox – simultaneously calm, slow, and ordinary whilst also hot, fast, and continuous – ecstatic, relentless, extra-ordinary. I feel the Divine – which I perceive in this instance to be the cosmic energy of inspiration – as an actual part of the fabric of my being – embedded in my neurons and vocal cords. We are one and the same.

I have had to learn how to balance the embodied experience of writing and teaching. If I don't it 'burns me'. By that, I mean it can fatigue me, as the lifeforce energy activated within me when I put pen to paper or speak to groups runs faster than my body can process, whether that be speaking, typing, or writing. I know I'm not alone in this, as other creatives have experienced this phenomenon.

I have discovered that this Divine, erotic, creative energy can lead to burnout if not channelled in a way that the nervous system and physiology can integrate. I could sit and talk, write or type what the erotic wants me to express, engaging and embodying archetype of Oracle or Prophetess for hours on end – without rest – but I have learned that this is not sustainable. I will share more about this in the creativity section of the workbook.

Conversely, during the periods of my life when I have not been communing ecstatically with word in this sacred and erotic way I have experienced lifelessness, depression, and chronic fatigue. Word smithery, art and creativity are an erotic life-enhancing and nourishing processes. They feed me. Creating love through the Divine channel and alchemy of words is part of my heartbeat and circulation. And as someone once said to me – I am in fact a 'word witch'.

There are words which come through me or from a deep part of self which I feel is beyond 'me'. I am fairly gentle and highly sensitive, and yet in ecstatic and erotic flow Divine words which move through my hand onto the computer screen and paper are words which 'I' would never say or my mind could never have thought. They can trigger, disrupt, and cause unease in the readers. This oracular and prophetic energy is not well received in the paradigm of this world. I would not consciously and willingly choose to inhabit a place where I create uneasiness. It's the very opposite of how I want to live – in harmony. And yet that unease is how I know the words are sacred and erotic – and truth.

Sacred words represent aliveness and lifeforce and are beyond convention and nicety. This book, for example, does not sit easy with the 'I'. Even the title itself is judged by my sensitivity and gentleness as 'too much', 'disruptive' and 'unnecessary'. But the erotic power and charge with which this book was birthed was from the oracular divine aspect of Self. I had no choice – it was gestating and would be birthed whether I liked it or not. I was to speak, write, and share – regardless of the ego's discomfort – as prophetess of the sanctity of embodiment and the holiness of flesh. I watched the words spontaneously type themselves out onto the screen – 'the visioning of collective evolution through metacognition, embodiment and creativity, and the amalgamation of metacognition, intuition and instinct'. This was an ecstatic experience, a sacred message and pledge delivered through inspired erotic word. I find it best to express what I receive, feel, see, and know without analysis. I find it best to just keep writing. If I try to make sense or justify it all, I simply get a keen sense that what I am writing is simply truth.

So, *what is inspiration?*

According to www.dictionary.com, it is 'an inspiring or animating action or influence: something inspired, as an idea, a result of inspired activity, a thing or person that inspires. Theology: a divine influence directly and immediately exerted upon the mind or soul, the divine quality of the writings or words of a person so influenced. The drawing of air into the lungs; inhalation'.

The origin of the word is the Latin *inspirare;* 'in' (inside) *'spirare'* (to breathe). Through inspiration we dive deeply into the divinity within us and inhale the Divine through our breath, oxygenating and enlivening our blood with Divine aliveness, enhancing the words we express. Interestingly, breath is often considered Spirit, which is also referred to as lifeforce, which in relation to this book is the erotic.

Breath and word have often been associated with the Divine and sacred. *Logos*, the Greek word for word, is associated with knowledge. For Christians, *Logos* is the action through which things are made divine (Jesus in John's Gospel being the Word incarnating into human form). Word and breath then are aspects of the Divine which both flow into and out of humans through inspired, ecstatic, sacred embodiment and experiences. Writers and poets make love with the Divine this way.

Certainly, there have been times in my life where I could only have produced the quality and quantity of the written words in relation to Divine flow. I completed my MA part-time, with three young children in nine months. I was intoxicated, ecstatically in love with the learning, co-creating innovative ideas, theological thought in tandem with eros and inspiration. It was easy. There was no force; the words flowed through and from me – I just surrendered, allowed, and watched the process of my divine mind make love and make manifest on the page.

Words themselves hold divine and sacred power – sounding them verbally creates a deeper ecstatic and erotic experience (more of this next month). Sacred acts and witchcraft have long activated and channelled Divine union through a sigil – the creation of a magical symbolic word from the words of an intention in order to manifest a desired outcome. So is the power of enchanted sacred writing that is infused with erotic power.

Writing with devotion is a sacred process. Love making and expression through literature and poetry is common and devotional. Sacred poetry is best exemplified in the mystic and thirteenth century Persian poet Rumi's work. His writing expresses an internal love making with the Divine. He writes 'your task is not to seek love, but merely to seek and find all the barriers within yourself that you built against it'. We, as the participants said in the interviews, 'open up' to it.

The sacred word – truth – has a particular tone and quality. It comes from beyond logic, analysis, empiricism. It just is. It is life moving through the pen or keyboard. When I am writing words of truth, they are sure, precise, non-aggressive, clear. They are without judgement, criticism, or doubt. Discerning Divine truth in my words has reduced anxiety and given me confidence to express. I feel that when we read truth, we recognise the lifeforce of the writer in the words and the love-weave they have created with their Divine essence. One of the best examples of erotic word in which aliveness, lifeforce, is palpable – and the ecstatic power of the Divine explodes through her expression on the page – is the poem *Still I Rise* by Maya Angelou. The erotic and hypnotic heartbeat of the repeated words, '*Still I Rise*' is the power of her love making with the Divine and burns untruth to the ground.

Art by Arna Baartz

Try this: Sacred journaling of the WORD

W What guidance are you requesting?
O Open invitation
R Receive
D Download

The purpose of this practise is to access and strengthen your connection with your Divine word and its tone. If you already journal this may be familiar already; the aim is to explore the love which can be birthed from it and the life which manifests through it.

For this month, set aside a minimum of ten minutes every day for you to commune and journal. Ideally this will be the same time, in the same place, with the same pen and notebook every day.

Make the preparations for the time slot of journaling a sacred ritual. It's good to have a pen and notebook which look and feel aesthetically pleasing to you. Try to sit in a space which is warm and comfortable – the lighting feels good for your nervous system and the seat is comfortable. Perhaps make an erotic hot drink (see month two) to have with you.

Pause. Look around the room. Feel your feet on the floor, back and bottom against the chair. Rest and allow your mind, body, and energy to reflect on what you would like to receive words on. You can simply ask for support in general, or on a specific issue or relationship. Or you might want to receive an answer to a question. You choose.

Write down the topic or question. Open and receive and then just write. Write, write, write words. Anything, everything. Observing and feeling the tone, where they originate from. Whether they are being written with ease or force. Keep going, do not stop for at least ten minutes.

When it feels complete, review the download. *What has been revealed?*

Eventually you will feel, see, hear, think, and know which words are flowing as a sacred stream, are eros, lifeforce, cocreated, woven with a divine strand or from divine origin – and which are programming, conditioning, and a regurgitation of what you have been taught by others. Your sacred word, your truth – has a particular quality to it. It may take a little while to become familiar and acquainted with it. By the end of this month's practice, you should be able to identify it.

Here are extra prompts for this practice.

Ideas of topics and questions to journal on:

- What is power?

- What is truth?

- What and where is safety?

- What does my body want me to know?

- How is my mind confusing me?

- What causes my anxiety?

- Why do I feel depressed?

- How can I feel alive again?

- What do I desire?

- What am I not seeing?

- Why am I confused?

- What does my teenage self want me to shout about?

- What am I hiding?

- What story is written in my heart?

- What words does my voice want to speak?

Engage the body:

- What can I see, hear, taste, smell, touch?

- Why do I feel pain where I do?

- What is the reason I am experiencing x?

- What does my womb want me to know?

- What are my eyes closed to?

- Why am I not speaking?

Use the space below for any additional thoughts.

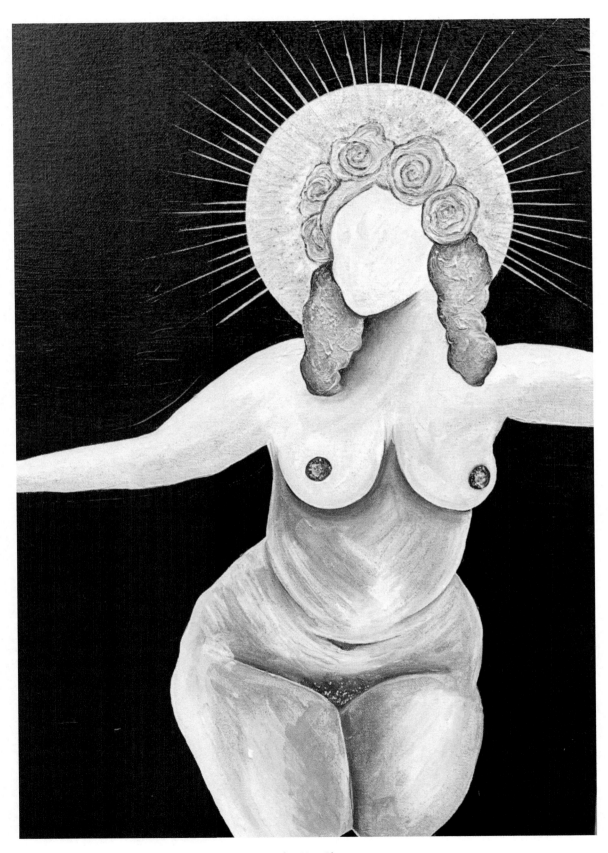

Art by Kat Shaw

Month 4
Theme: Sound

'Anything human can be felt through music, which means that there is no limit to the creating that can be done with music. You can take the same phrase from any song and cut it up so many different ways – it's infinite. It's like God... you know?'
–Nina Simone

'Does not wisdom call out?
Does not understanding raise her voice?

Listen, for I have trustworthy things to say;
I open my lips to speak what is right.

My mouth speaks what is true,
for my lips detest wickedness'.

–Proverbs 8

Discussion:

As a baby grows in its mother's womb, the sense of sound is fully activated. We develop in a cacophony cocoon hearing the sound of the wash of blood circulating, digestive action, thumping heartbeat and our mother's voice, as well as the muffled day-to-day sounds outside of her body. The baby receives this sound through their acumen of hearing, their ears, but also through feeling, through vibration and frequency, transmitted and reverberating through the mother's bones and fluids. Our first connection of that which is other than self, and yet fully connected to self, is through sound. The first love we make is through sound, through hearing and connecting and through feeling and connecting.

Frequency and vibes (vibration) are terms associated with music and sound. We hear frequencies, we sense them, but we also feel them, and they can have a massive impact on mood, emotions, and consciousness – and can elicit highly charged and deeply relaxing, sacred, erotic, and ecstatic states and connection. Although scientists and sound practitioners may be able to explain the exact maths and Hz in relation to which frequency or sound universally impacts the brain and consciousness in specifically upbeat or detrimental ways (as in the case of sound torture or brainwashing), this book is not going into sound at that depth.

The focus this month is to explore how sounds and the energy of sounds support us to feel alive, weaving love, connected to that which is beyond the mundane and yet, infused within it and also ecstatic. While there may be some similarity in the collective responses gathered for this month, sounds were experienced as sacred and connected the participant to their sense of divinity. Each was a uniquely individual experience.

The topic of conversational sound elicited an immense variety of responses amongst respondents in how sacred speech was defined and interpreted. For some it was a whisper, and gentle, for others impassioned and loud. Some women were happy with arguments and felt an erotic force, aliveness move through them during this – that the Divine was within the conflict – even swearing. For others this was not ok and disconnected them fully from connection with their own lifeforce, and any Divine weaving.

Certainly, holy anger, activism, and advocacy through the sound of speaking personal truth for me is a highly erotic and sacred experience of making love with the Divine. It is a paradox that I feel most connected to Divine love through words – writing and speaking – and yet it is in conversation, that I have struggled most with personal confidence and also have experience the most. I am introverted and quiet, neurodivergent, and still find the frequency and vibration of shouting, critical words, and sarcasm more destructive and threatening to my erotic lifeforce and spirit than physical threat. At school and in university I was painfully shy in class and did everything I could to avoid speaking or reading aloud. If I were asked to answer questions or give my opinion I would blush and shake. I still do not particularly like being 'seen' or speaking publicly – but I will do it on behalf of injustice, and to represent those who have experienced abuse and neglect. And I have always found teaching, creating affirming and safe group dynamics, and sharing an extremely easeful and a sacred process.

I feel the frequency and vibration of the Divine most strongly when I allow flow, eros, lifeforce, to speak through written word and voice. My biggest wounds – the loss or diminishment of my voice, chronic shyness and gaslighting, have ironically transformed and healed and become powerful channels for lovemaking with the Divine. I can confidently and powerfully, without experiencing doubt, speak sacred and erotic words of love and connection when facilitating. My voice, words and truth all carry erotic power and through them when I make ecstatic, earth-quaking Love with the Divine. I have recognised 'the power of the erotic within our lives can give us the energy to pursue genuine change within our world', Audre Lorde. I blaze brightly vocally and speak with wisdom, the embodiment of the current of Feminine captured within the archetype of the Goddess Sophia. 'My mouth speaks what is true', and as a channel of Divine frequency, I have courage and strength that is not there when I am not connected to that flow of eros and inspiration. My sacred voice – my physical vocal cords – are being played by the Divine musician. The performance is love.

Singers can transform lyrics, word poems, into ecstatic offerings. The marriage of words and music offers us a Divine portal to the ecstatic and erotic. Songs and music can move us and shift our own personal frequency into the sacred, ecstatic, erotic and joyful instantaneously. Women talked about feeling 'oneness' through music, 'restored' and 'felt' by something other than them through music. For me, power ballads never fail. Equally I feel a deep connectedness, peace, belonging and love when singing in a choir – that our voices blend, weave, love make and birth a new divine sound of oneness. Research showed me though that there was a wide variety of music which does this. When asked which music made them feel fully alive and connected to the Divine, answers given by participants ranged from choral, opera and classical (Mozart, Wagner and Beethoven were mentioned) to rap and dance – and to folk, traditional Irish and acoustic music. Some mentioned hymns, mantra, and chanting. It was highly individual. One participant explained that she believed our choice of music is different because we are 'different vibrations' and what 'inspires us is according to our own vibration'.

There can be a specific song or piece of music which is a perfect match for our vibration and the Divine which results in a fully bodied love making experience and state. One of the most beautiful stories I had the privilege of hearing while researching this part of the book was a woman's account of her love of what she described as 'cheesy' musicals and the song storytelling of the hero/heroine initiation and life dance. One of her favourites was *West Side Story*. She described how the song, 'There is a place for us' was an aspect of one of her most profound fully human and fully divine love making moments. She recalled a memory of being in the bath whilst her partner was outside. The radio was on, and this song came on. Without being prompted, quite spontaneously her partner came to the bathroom and as she walked to the doorway saw his hand out. He had come to dance with her to this song. She described this moment, the symbiosis of the song, the lyrics, the sentiment, the emotion, his spontaneity, the synchronicity as 'ecstatic, erotic and beautiful'. She felt there was archetypical energies at play. There was something 'simple and profound' being 'channelled through us' she said, and we were 'two becoming one'. She was surprised at the overwhelming and emotional power of the memory of this. I too wept as she told the story – the Divine has made love through them and then through her storytelling to me.

Drumming, and the seven basic vowel sounds especially, were described as sounds which facilitated embodied union with the Divine, changing brainwave states and supporting journeying and altered and meditative states of consciousness. One woman described how drumming and movement (more about this next month) vibrated through her body, activating ecstatic orgasmic pulsations. I have found that drumming, sounding with my own voice as voo, ahh, om, oo, oh, and ah in deeper tones and a root chakra pitched sound bowl vibrations activate an embodied and physical pulsation at the perineum which activates an erotic flow of lifeforce energy through both my chakra system, and spine – my nervous system and into my womb space. It feels as though I am making love with the Divine at an anatomical, cellular, and vibrational level with the beat and frequency.

Some participants noted that gong baths allowed them to connect and weave with the Divine, experiencing sacred, ecstatic, and erotic states. Descriptions of mystical and ecstatic experiences during gong baths included 'feelings of being held or merging with Light beings', 'floating in the cosmos', 'communication with the moon', experiencing communications and guidance from star beings and plants, 'edging with the sound waves and becoming fluid form'. One participant described the sacred experience of a spontaneous soul retrieval, activated by the vibrations of the gong during which an aspect of her soul 'came to me like a light in my heart – a portal opened, and I experienced a warm glow'. She continued, stating that as the frequency of the gong intensified, she continued the journey and the soul part 'raised her palm to mine and I felt her compassion – she knew I would embrace her and carry her with me in my core'.

My own experience of a mystical experience during sound therapy included receiving geometric energetic patterning and gridding. During one gong bath I experienced an ecstatic and mystical embodied moment during which my energy system and lifeforce merged with that of my husband in sacred geometric formations and shapes. The weaving and love making seemed to be happening as a six-part process in this instance, orchestrated and conducted by the Divine. The process was as follows: (1) The Divine directed sacred frequency, vibration, and energy, through the channel of the sound healer's body, and then (2) through her gongs, (3) into the air waves and energy of this realm (4) into my body (5) and the body of my husband (6) to weave our energy bodies to create a matrix of a sacred template.

This sound healer described how 'sound is a force they (Spirit) can work with to raise our vibration, to assist our development and realise our potential. She explained, 'I am currently working with the Goddess Isis; she is very connected to the frequencies of the gongs offer'. She also emphasised the importance of opening and receptivity. She felt, like the writers in the earlier chapter, that a force, a flow – which is beyond her – weaves through her physicality, her body, to support her sound work. In this weave and love making, she experiences sacred, erotic, and ecstatic states. She explained, 'I have found that it is best to let energies work through me and the gong. It is certainly more comfortable to open up and succumb to the divine lava of love'. How delicious is that phrase – 'divine lava of love'.

Try this: Spell out LIFE

Our voice, the sound it makes, can often be something we diminish, hide, or 'quieten'. We also can 'minimise' or not speak our full truth. Giving life to and speaking into being our desires, wants and needs is powerful. Spelling out vocally what we want activates an erotic energy, it gives the words life – animates them, moves them from thought into reality – in speaking our desires we move the vibration from thought and internal embodiment into form in the world. Hence the phrase 'casting a spell' which is a verbal formula, the frequency of moving love, longing, or desire from thought and through words and actioning them into life and reality. A spell is words with erotic power, lifeforce – a union of the power of human will and divine will – love making and birthing into life.

So, this month your practice is to experience the power of the sound, vibration and frequency of your truth, voice, and energy. You are going to spell out and birth your LIFE.

Every day this month, ideally at the start of each day, you are going to spend five minutes speaking or singing aloud what your desires and longing are for that day. You can have the same desire for each day of the month or change the desire every day – whatever feels good and is easiest for you to commit to. You can do this in the bathroom for example, in the shower at the start of the day.

Each day complete and speak or sing aloud three times these sentences.

'Today I choose LIFE'

L Let me receive …
I Invite more of …
F From my relationships I choose …
E Every moment I will …

It is really powerful to do this whilst looking in the mirror and even more powerful to voice or video record yourself on your phone saying these words and noticing how every day your lifeforce and erotic power grow. Recording yourself and playing it back throughout the day increases the love making and flow of Divine through your life and embodiment.

If you are singing the words, it is a good idea to initially sing a nursery rhyme tune that is familiar and light-hearted as it brings an erotic playfulness to the practice. You can also experiment singing the words in different genres and styles of music to see which brings the words more alive to you and makes you feel embodied. This will connect you to a style of music through which ecstasy and the erotic unites with your own frequency and vibration. Try singing the words in the style of rock, opera, rap, pop, classical, and chanting as a starting point.

Art by Arna Baartz

Month 5

Theme: Movement

'Everything in the universe has a rhythm, everything dances'.
–Maya Angelou

'Movement never lies. It is a barometer telling the state of the soul's weather to all who can read it'.
–Martha Graham

'Dancers are the messengers of the gods'.
–Martha Graham

Discussion:

Sacred movement within ceremony and ritual dancing healing, prayers and gratitude, and embodied meditation, have been part of spiritual practice and religions throughout all the human timeline of existence. It is through movement that our animal, our human, our flesh, bones, muscles animate – give life and embodied existence to the Divine. The sacred animals that we are, dance the Divine out and into this physical realm of earth.

Within Shamanic practice, the oldest spiritual phenomenon known to humankind with unique lineages prevalent in all cultures – ecstatic trance dance and movement, shapeshifting into movements and embodying the physical form of power animals and animal archetypes – is a normal occurrence. Through ecstatic and trance states (facilitated through vibrational and energetic shifts by drumming, movement, and dance) the Shaman is able to weave, commune and bridge ordinary reality – earth realm – and the Spirit and Divine realm for individual, community and collective healing.

My personal experiences of this are many and wide ranging. The most prevalent are the shapeshifting experiences into the archetypes of Serpent and Jaguar. Each have their own bespoke sacred sensation and frequency. When I embody Jaguar, I am moving as and with the Divine protectress, huntress and can unite with the lifeforce of sacred, holy anger, gaining clarity of boundaries. I feel her inhabit my body, claws, arched back, ready to pounce and hunt, her snarl and growl ready to speak to injustice. She pulses through the current of sympathetic nervous system activation – healthy fight – but offers an embodied shapeshifting sacred dimension to my own animal human self: discernment. Jaguar is the Divine and ecstatic manifestation in my form of the sovereign, queen, warrioress Sacred feminine. She is wise, ancient, volcanic.

Serpent, within my body, is the Divine current of the erotic – the kundalini, lifeforce and earth energy – which spontaneously moves my animal self into flow, through spirals, circular movements, and undulation. I feel the presence of a double helix serpent in my nervous system and DNA, ecstatically and tantrically weaving divinity and humanity as one within me. Serpent is also the energy of eros, the erotic lifeforce fire moving through my body and powering orgasmic ecstasy. She also feels like a sacred feminine energy – one of lover, mother, and nurturer. I have created love and huge shifts in my life – weaving realities with these archetypes, in an embodied way.

Serpent and kundalini were the focus of many shares in relation to making love with the divine through movement. One participant shared a verbal account of an unexpected, fully embodied, visceral, and deeply erotic and ecstatic experience of lovemaking with the Divine whilst on retreat. The combination of dance, music and the heat and humidity of the sacred temazcal hot stones in the yurt was erotically weaving serpent into her embodied awareness and experience. She described that during the ceremony, as the heat kept building, she held the clear intention of 'show me – show me'. She freely moved her body. Allowing life itself to move both into and through her, from within her and out of her. The erotic aliveness danced through every atom, muscle, bone, and limb of her body. As she travelled ever deeper into her animal body and out of the logical mind – her consciousness altered. She had a vision of 'a fat silvery serpent' and felt the 'ecstatic sensations of bliss' which she described as 'orgasmic', and which began to 'fuel wave after wave' of 'sensual and divine' sensation within her.

This was not expected and neither had it been tutored. She was experiencing a spontaneous mystical and ecstatic lovemaking with the Divine, through Serpent, within her animal body. She described that whilst she knew others were in the tent with her, she was in her own unique, intimate, and private union with an 'electrifying lifeforce' and was in 'pure connection with light and blissfulness'. This 'light energy and purity' she said is 'how we are meant to be as women'. She was clearly changed forever by this mystical and numinous experience and declared, 'I am the bridge to bliss and healing, to sensation and freedom, which heals as we dance to the truth'. She also knowingly expressed that this erotic, divine power had always been with her because in her younger life she had felt it was 'dangerous to dance' and that 'boyfriends had dragged her off the dancefloor'. I got the sense from her that would never happen again and that she was now an advocate of the Divine power and sacredness of a woman's body dancing the erotic.

This woman's experience vocalises the fear many religions had of the power of woman's body and dance as a direct link and union with the Divine. Ecstatic movement is the highway – a direct line of communication with God/Goddess/Spirit and that is why in some religions dance was banned and/or controlled within worship. One participant talked about how she experienced 'dance dancing through her' – which had taken her by surprise. The mind is not involved, and she described it as the dancing that comes from 'within her body' – lifeforce emanating out from her. We can see how empowering that is. It is not only a direct embodied union with the Divine, but also indicates that we are the Divine – we are the source of aliveness, spirit, lifeforce. We do not need anything external to us to know that we are holy, sacred, and Divine. No priests, gurus, teachers, holy books, dogmas, or doctrine are needed.

Intellect and qualifications are inconsequential. Woman's body is the source of Divine, lifeforce, the sacred. It is revolutionary.

One research participant described how this creative innate Divine force and union has nothing to do with intelligence. Making love with the Divine she said is, 'ultimate connection'. She explained that 'it is a direct experience when I am completely in the moment'. She continued saying, 'I experience it most when I am dancing predominantly with dancers who have profound and multiple learning difficulties. We drop into a world beyond words where only that moment matters and, in that moment, we are one – it blows my mind'.

Getting out of the mind through movement was a point made by several participants as essential for love making with the Divine and accessing sacred, erotic, and ecstatic experiences. As previous months have explained, an aspect of this phenomena is about opening up and receiving – coming into the no-mind, flow state, letting aliveness, spirit, the divine, flow, lead and move you. Slowing and stilling or 'calming the mind' through 'yoga physical postures' allows for embodied union, or as one woman described, 'an experience of the spiritual' to happen.

How women did this with movement varied. One woman shared that mindfully walking helped. Another described her 'morning run in the sunshine' felt like love making with the Divine and was a time she felt most alive. For me personally, swimming elicits this without fail. The sensation of water on my skin, the silky, flowing movements of my body gliding weightlessly through the water is a super-charged, fully embodied, non-cerebral union of myself and the Divine in the element of water, co-creating ease, grace, fluidity, and flow.

One of the women I received contributions from as part of the research was a seasoned wild swimmer. Her experience of flow was amplified by the setting of nature which erotically charged the love making (which will be the focus of next month). Her share states, 'outdoor swimming is more than exercise or cold water for me. It connects me to the feminine within – shapeshifting, free flowing, ever-changing. I dance in her waters, absorbing every moment of beauty around me, completely connected to my body. Swimming in the river has connected me into my body like nothing else, once you are in, there is no space to think about anything else but how it feels. It brings on feelings of extreme joy, happiness, calm and awe at the natural landscape. We are no longer human and river, but one, interconnected. Becoming one with nature is something I now practice daily through wild swimming, walks in the wood and gardening'.

Erotic energy is an untamed, unmatched, powerful force of creativity which births through destruction, death, and rebirth. And it is generated in a woman's movement and the earth. Women's bodies in movement both create and channel it. One woman shared that she creates with the Divine when she 'moves, dances and cries'. She 'sees' this creative force as 'powerful spirals and pulsating energy'. The pulsation of the erotic, and spiral swirling were adjectives used repeatedly in the research descriptions. The body is the dwelling place, home, vessel, sanctuary for the Divine and through which erotic ecstasy is experienced. World religions do have a tradition of circular dance – circle dance in the Anglican Christian Church is a moving meditation, whilst Shaktism in Hinduism and Sufi Islam Whirling Dervish dance are more ecstatic.

One participant shared at length about her experiences of erotic kundalini, snake, and belly dance movements. How this links with her witchcraft will be discussed in later months. Her regular, solo, loving making process with the Divine in the form of the Goddess Shakti and Lilith was activated through raising kundalini. She explained that belly dance connects us to our sacred womb and creative energy. It supports pain management, sexual and sensual expression. Here is her practice:

'I spiral my lower body, then solar plexus and then top chakras, using words or chants to awaken the energy and bring it up through my body. I call Lilith and ask her to embody me, move inside of me to awaken kundalini. I chant to get out of the mental space. This is more meditative than the average process. I am in a state of no thought for longer periods of time. Lilith, sometimes as moonlight, moves inside of me through my vagina and my entire core. I ask her to assist me in pleasure, orgasm and assist kundalini. As I do that my body spontaneously moves. My belly and hips rotate, and I perform undulations, snake-like movements, belly dance and move side to side to awaken the spine energy. Movements come spontaneously to me when Lilith is invoked. My hands move like wings as she guides. Once I achieve orgasm, the energy is so strong that I give grateful thanks and offer excess energy to the Goddess Freya at my altar and to the Earth for healing and crops. More recently I have channelled the energy into poetry or sound. This is an intuitive process. Working with Goddess and raising kundalini has helped my physically and emotionally. I experience happiness and satisfaction internally. This energy flow has created great joy in my life, and I am singing all the time. I feel abundant without any lack both physically and spiritually. I no longer have a sense of longing for anyone or anything outside myself, as I feel complete and satisfied very deep down within my soul'.

Art by Arna Baartz

Try this: Find and move with your own unique Divine rhythm

This month is about you exploring how you make love with the Divine through movement. This is an experiential practice of curiosity and discovery. These details are simply a prompt and stimulus.

Preparation:

Start by taking a moment to reflect and journal on these questions:

1. *Have you ever experienced a time in the past when you:*

    - *Felt your body was being moved by life or a force/energy which was beyond you?*

    - *Were moving fluidly and easefully, without stress?*

    - *Felt your body was totally in flow?*

If you answered yes write down what you were doing, what happened and what it felt like.

2. *What sort of movement do you prefer and why?* (e.g., Fast or slow? Staccato or fluid? Dancing? Running? Walking? Yoga? Swimming?)

Now produce a 10–15-minute playlist of songs which feel and sound so good that your body automatically wants to move to them.

Practice:

For 15 minutes each day, go to a space where you will not be disturbed. When you arrive in the space take a few minutes to orient yourself.

Set and speak aloud every day – before you begin – the intention to allow the erotic, the Divine, lifeforce (use whatever word feels good to you) move and weave love through your body during today's movement.

Put on the playlist and allow your body to move as it wants to.

Here are some suggestions for variation and experimentation throughout the month. See what happens if:

- During the first 3 minutes of the practice shake your body and then move.

- You move outside rather than inside.

- You move in the dark rather than light, night rather than daytime.

- For the first 5 minutes you rotate your hips only.

- For the first 3 minutes you stand absolutely still.

- You are menstruating.

- You change the word of your intention, e.g., one day to allow the erotic, another day to allow the Divine, another day to allow lifeforce, etc.

- You move without intention.

- You move with someone else in the space.

- You move without music.

- You miss a day.

- You invite Serpent to move with or through you.

- You invite another God/Goddess/archetype/being to move with or through you.

- You move as water.

- You move as fire.

- You move as air.

- You move to the rhythm of the earth.

- You set the intention and go for a walk instead.

- You lie down.

- You set the intention and go running instead.

If you have any other adaptations you want to try, please do! The aim is to move with your eros, aliveness, Divine lifeforce.

Complete the month journaling an answer to this sentence starter:

The Divine moves into, within and through me by …

Art by Katie Kavanagh

Month 6
Theme: Nature

'The Word is living, being, spirit, all verdant greening, all creativity. This Word manifests itself in every creature'.
–Hildegard of Bingen

'Nature will come and make love to you'.
–Rev Rowan Bombadil, 'Ecosensual Awakening' in *Igniting Intimacy: Sex magic rituals for practical living and loving*

Discussion:

Nature is our natural habitat, the territory of the human animal that we are. Our mammal strongly resonates with wildlife, flora, and fauna. Being in the wild connects us fully and deeply, at a non-cognitive level with all creatures and the whole natural world. We connect and feel into the unique vibrations and frequencies of all aspects and classification of nature and sentient being. One participant said that from her time in nature, 'I realise how everything that is natural is sacred from the earth and universe'. Another woman expressed that although, 'I vibrate at a different frequency than a stone, it doesn't mean that I am better'.

Connecting to the consciousness, energy and divinity of the whole natural world is one way we make love, weave, and unite with the Divine. One woman told me the story of being on 'on edge of Costa Rican jungle, on a high platform, looking down and I'd become part of it all; the soaring Eagle; the lush greenery; the sky. Later Hawk came into the dining room and sat on chair. It turned around and we made deep connection. I wasn't sure where I ended, and it began'.

Nature and the Earth itself supply us with life itself, eros. The Divine makes love to us erotically in this way – moving up from the Earth, through our body and chakras – with the loving purpose of expansion and wellness. Bathing in nature engages our parasympathetic nervous system and so brings our entire system into a rest, relaxation, and creative state. Abbess, mystic, writer, and medical practitioner Hildegard of Bingen (c 1098-1179) wrote about Viriditas, the greening Divine energy and a force which enlivens both the soul and body. The participant who shared the Costa Rica narrative above, continued with her storytelling and explained, 'I attempt to consciously connect with lifeforce, intertwining with it throughout my day. These moments are my oxygen. I realise I am a tiny part of a magical whole. These moments mostly occur in nature'.

Another woman explained her experience in more detail, describing how for her the erotic is a teacher – from which she learns and develops – and in connection with the earth is empowered. She shared that 'for me personally this is the erotic universal energy and is something I feel vibrationally and unconditionally. It flows, it nurtures, and it makes me question everything. It teaches me if I am willing to let it – mainly through the blockages! It always blocks in the areas that I need to let go. When I feel it and let it flow and connect with it via earth energy, it makes me feel invincible, beautiful, and peaceful. My head gets a rest, my logical mind drains down into the core of Mama Earth'. This description beautifully explains the divine, nurturing, loving and symbiotic relating and life enhancing weave of woman's body and nature's body.

The Divine love making which happens through nature and within our energy and physical bodies, was described by participants as being centralised on the sacral and womb – our pleasure and creative centre. Nature weaves erotically into our emotions and sexual energy. Being in the wild stirs up the womb and activates powerful sensations in that gestational and birthing space. Women shared that in nature they experience twinges, stirrings, and expansion in their space. One share expressed a woman's 'love to connect to nature – seeds, feathers, leaves and medicinal herbs'. She explained that she brings them into her body 'and absorbs their unique qualities or ingest into my soul'. Another woman described that an 'electric feeling in sacral chakra comes alive when I look at patterns of a feather, or creation and power of soul'.

My own experiences of connecting to the earth – the heat of the sun, or coldness of natural water, the warm breeze and damp, moist earth – are focalised directly on the relationship between the elements and bare skin. Having my body, semi-naked, on the earth and outside in the elements is a deeply erotic, ecstatic, and sacred experience of love making with the Divine. Although my whole skin is impacted through this unity, the strongest connection and activation always happens in the root and sacral, specifically the perineum and vulva. I had no idea others were having these mystical, lifeforce and Divine connections through nature this way until I read R Bombadil's book, *Igniting Intimacy: Sex magic rituals for practical living and loving*, whilst researching. In it they use the term ecosexuality, which encompasses practices which 'combine our individual eroticism and our natural environment'. They explain that we can connect to the Earth as a lover and be in relationship with it in a sexual and non-sexual erotic way.

I had already – untutored – laid in the sun and felt at both a conscious level, through intention, and at an unconscious level, the heat penetrate 'me' – my skin and chakras directly – creating an activation in eros, an intertwining of my energy and with the element of fire, deepening aliveness and the weave between my body, divine energy, and universal forces. Bombadil describes in her book that this is a practice that can be cultivated where we 'allow the sun to come to you in a form that arouses you'. Conscious love making with the Divine sun, co-creating with erotic earthly and cosmic lifeforce and libido. One woman I interviewed also described that 'when I am amongst trees and alone, I feel a primal power focused on my root and sacral, and at times it feels raw and sexual. Earth energy makes me feel like that; it is a dance with energies entwined and at the deepest core level'. We are experiencing ecosexuality, and as R. Bombadil so beautiful expresses, the 'earth as our love'.

It is a natural progression then for us to feel that natural objects found on walks are gifts from a lover, an energy which deeply wants and cherishes us and who is showering us with beautiful tokens of this bond. Items found on walks, beaches, and in forests, were considered precious, and many women expressed that they were of more value to them than bought items. Feathers were more precious than diamonds and cared for more carefully and reverently than jewellery. Certainly, for me the barn owl feather and this rock I found on a walk with my husband last summer is more special to me than any synthetic object I own. I felt the rock was a stone reflection of my Soul and energetic self – light and dark. I felt it was a message of support that my deepening into shadow work was vital, and as I examined it, I felt an erotic connection with my own path and that of humanity as a whole.

Two-way communication with nature was common and described in a variety of ways by contributors. Some, like me, saw objects found as messages from the Divine – metaphors to consider and receive wisdom from. Others felt plants and animals carried messages and energy to them. Several described whispers and verbal communication with nature, especially trees. Here is one woman's share in relation to this: 'very occasionally, in my 58 years, I have experienced what I feel are sacred moments. It is here that I would say aliveness moves through me. Walking in Cardiff, I heard the whispering of the trees, the breeze had a quality to it, a message. I felt like it was speaking to me; I froze to listen, as if I were downloading some secret information. Then it passed and everything seemed normal again. There have been other moments in my life when I suddenly understand everything, I see existence, life, the cosmos, in a flicker, and I suddenly understand the meaning of life. I see the essence of everything – all in a nano second. I am unable to hold it, it's not mine to keep, yet! It's as if some divine information just flowed through me for that tiny moment. Then it's gone'.

Another woman said that 'trees talk' to her, extending words of guidance and encouragement when she is running. One of the main messages she received was 'go gently, all things will come at the right time'. She described how she does energy practices whilst communing with a tree, torso and the trunk of the tree combining into an energetic flow in a unified way, which echoes Hildegaard's sentiment in her book *Scivias:* 'The soul circulates through the body like sap through a tree, maturing a person the way sap helps a tree turn green and grow flowers and fruit'. Nature speaks to us, this particular participant said. She went on to explain that different trees have different energies and their own unique embrace. Old trees can still be 'very youthful with energetic spirits. She described all trees as benevolent and nurturing. It is also the case for this participant that she feels trees really 'see her' and can sometimes 'stare at her'. Other women described how – like this experience of energy sharing with a tree – we always receive feedback when we communicate with nature. It is always reciprocated. Someone said that 'branches wave' and 'grasses caress our legs'. The communication we receive, according to the research, is always safe, affirming and erotic – lifeforce giving and nervous system regulating. Participants called this 'magic'. One participant stated that she makes love with the Divine during 'moments in nature where it will feel like unbound joy and mutual appreciation'.

One participant, who walks a nature-based pagan path, talked about the Goddess Danu and earthy fecundity and that the 'ancient living energy' innate to the land holds 'the wisdom of millennia' which cannot be eradicated.

She went on to describe that within nature, ecstatic and erotic moments are always accessible – for example, 'a leaf falling from a tree' or a 'beautiful sunset', which incidentally is one of the ways Carl Jung experienced the numinous. She explained how there are certain locations on earth where she recognises that her connection becomes stronger. These can correspond to areas where meridians and sacred ley and dragon lines of pure energy intersect the earth. They can be remote places, although many are sacred sites or have temples, churches or cathedrals built upon them. She goes there with her partner to 'plug in'. These areas of earth have 'supernatural powers' she said. In these locations there is more 'accessibility to the Divine and connection to spirit is amplified'. Her experiences here are 'visceral and palpable'. She goes to them to 'renew, restore and rejuvenate' and when there, she is always 'touched by the Divine is a special way'.

Being 'touched' by the Divine in nature was a theme described in many ways. Women shared that all the physical senses were 'touched', and that there was an energetic and mystical aspect to the experience. Being amongst trees and in woods raised kundalini and elicited erotic and deeply mystical experiences in many participants. Interconnectedness, oneness, profound emotionality, and love making with the sacred dimension of the earth was described. The divinity of the earth was universally safe and a space of safety, comfort, and regeneration. It was never a one-way process and so was an experience of being in an affirming and mutual relationship. It moved me to tears to hear and read descriptions such as this one: 'I have experiences in the wood which have made me feel alive in ways that no other times have. Times where I have purposefully connected in and communicated with Mother Earth. I've sent a root down to her heart and opened my crown to the energy of the universe, creating a green energy (visualised as a spinning green 3-D diamond) in my heart space. For me it is a form of communication, an opening, a remembering of the relationship and connectedness we have with nature. We are nature. I feel energy coursing throughout my body, the life-force of the universe. Revitalised, I have a keen sense of belonging and being held. Nature has become my safe space. After such experiences I receive blessings from the earth in the form of beautiful feathers or an abundance of doors opening/ connection with others. At times, these blessings have been so special to me that they have brought me to tears. They have reminded me that we are all one and at the same time have given me a sense of belonging. I am realising that these messages and this relationship has been there all my life, but I have never taken the time to slow down, connect and see it'. Notice again the descriptions of reciprocity, ecstasy, lifeforce and 'greening' energy, which Hildegard wrote about.

The healing, protective and trauma-releasing, and containment power of nature's touch was powerfully expressed by one participant who courageously shared that she had a history of childhood sexual abuse and rape and so was unable to be touched by or trust humans. I was humbled and in awe that she expressed that she remained connected to 'magical' energy within the four elements and nature as a child, from which she received Divine comfort. She described this as 'pantheistic' (which is the word describing that God, the Divine, is in everything – inseparable from reality). She explained that as a child she could be safe and touched within water where she will 'float and stay in as long as possible, insulated, cradled and hugged'. She climbed trees also to be 'cradled and supported' and noticed that individual trees had 'different energies. She loved her 'hug tree'. She felt a pagan calling and found in nature the 'safe touch I was looking for'. She has received sacred, erotic, and ecstatic relating and Divine touch when 'going outside naked at night', when she 'stood on mountains' and while 'standing outside during a storm'.

Outdoor, day-to-day, and mundane life tasks such as gardening, were described as sacred practices, through which the Divine weaves symbiotically and creates love with us. One woman expressed that when she is in her 'veg plot or wandering fields, amongst the plants and in nature, gathering her abundance, I feel alive. In weeding and watering her earth – I'm nourishing myself'. There is no separation. This participant did share that she experienced overwhelm and a dissolution of her physical form, when she blended and merged with nature and cosmos simultaneously. Her union with the Divine appeared to be through cosmic consciousness in this description: 'I experience an intense overwhelming feeling of looking at the night sky and when I acknowledge an overall force. A power so strong it affects my physical body, like the sensation of rollercoaster. At other times, these spine-tingling moments, these connection with Spirit – left me silent'.

Foraging – receiving from the earth love and Divine nurturance throughout the seasons – brings us into deepening relationship, reciprocity, and gratitude with the earth. This is foundational to the most ancient human spiritual practices, shamanism, and paganism. Working in relationship with the elements of earth, air, fire, and water (plus ether, spirit, breath) are integral in weaving and union with the Divine. Alchemy and manifestation occur from right relationship and gratitude with the earth. Certainly, I personally weave and cocreate with the Divine when I offer gifts (such as sugar, water, honey, feathers and so on) to the earth, to an outdoor fire, and or to a natural body of water, most especially a sacred well near my home. Connecting to the body of the earth as the body of a great mother from whom we receive all sustenance, brings us into mystical union and oneness and an interdependence.

Art by Kat Shaw

Try this: Your body and the body of the Earth

This month's practice is about you creating a relationship between your body and the Earth, with the intention to explore a felt sense of the Divinity and love making within this. You can adjust the practice according to the season of the year.

The key is to connect your body and five senses to the four elements (air, water, fire, and earth) which make up nature – outside – and to feel what occurs as you do that. Notice what you see, feel, know, hear, and receive about making love with the Divine through the connection.

- Palms of hands (sense of touch)
- Eyes open (sense of sight)
- Mouth open (sense of taste)
- Listening (sense of hearing)
- Deep inhalation (sense of smell)

Week 1

Light a fire outside if autumn/winter or go outside on a sunny day if spring/summer.

Sit and place palms up to sunlight or towards flames of fire.

Feel sensation and energy of fire weave with your skin and energy.

Inhale the smell of fire and nature.

Open your mouth and taste fire and nature.

Listen to fire and nature.

Watch the fire or sunlight on grass/trees (do not look directly at the sun!)

Week 2

Go to an outside body of water – sea, river, well. Make sure it is free flowing.

Sit and immerse your hands in the water.

Feel sensation and energy of water weave with your skin and energy.

Inhale the smell of water and nature.

Open your mouth and taste water and nature.

Listen to water and nature.

Watch water flow.

Week 3

Go outside on a windy day.

Sit and place palms up against the flow of wind.

Feel the sensation and energy of airwaves on your skin.

Inhale the smell of air and nature.

Open your mouth and taste air and nature.

Listen to air and nature.

Watch the wind and air moving.

Week 4

Go outside on a day after it has been raining.

Sit and place palms onto soil.

Feel sensation and energy of earth weave with your skin and energy.

Inhale the smell of earth and nature.

Open your mouth and taste earth and nature.

Listen to earth and nature.

Watch the earth – notice quality, characteristic and colour.

Take a moment to write down some of your observations.

Art by Arna Baartz

Month 7

Theme: Creating

'Everybody born comes from the Creator trailing wisps of glory. We come from the Creator with creativity. I think that each one of us is born with creativity.'
–Maya Angelou

'There are no rules to creativity'.
–Laura Jaworski

Discussion:

Creating is an action during which, according to the Oxford Learner's Dictionary, we 'make, create or prepare something by combining materials or putting parts together; to cause something to exist or happen'. Throughout time, artists, writers, designers and indeed all other creatives, have described that creating starts with inspiration. They may have a muse who is there to activate this, or to provide the longing to create something, but the moment of inspiration – the receiving of the idea, the concept, the image – is always beyond them'. It is a force and influence which is generated elsewhere but is channelled through them. Inspiration 'drops in' and activates what Barbara Carrellas describes in her book *Ecstasy is Necessary* as 'the ecstatic mind' which is 'bright, undisturbed, full of potential, lit' and is a two-way lovemaking practice of creating and birthing something beautiful and meaningful.

For some, creating is a sacred operation. Inspiration originates from the Divine and is offered to the creative as a 'gift' or 'mission'. The ensuing crafting of the idea into form is done with devotion and reverence. One participant, an artist, described that her art and Priestessing (her feminine leadership and service) are one and the same. When she paints, she is serving the Divine, who for her is Goddess. She offered this description 'Priestess Artist' of the process:

'And I flung my head backwards, howling to the moon.
Goddess – how can I serve you?
Her reply was instantaneous.
'You are my Priestess.
Your power is your paintbrush.
Open up to me fully.
Surrender.
Let me enter you.
Allow me flow through your veins.
Quiver at my touch.
Feel me completely.
Know me intimately.
And then – Empower women, 1 body at a time'
–Words by Kat Shaw

This artist is also describing the creating process as an erotic 'know me intimately' and ecstatic 'let me enter you – allow me to flow through your veins – quiver at my touch – feel me completely' experience. There is a complete union and merging with the divine through her creating process. The love she makes is the empowerment of women. Naomi Wolf in her book *Vagina* expresses that 'women artists, writers, and revolutionaries' appear to follow the same patterns which she describes as 'a flowing of creative insight and vision' that 'seemed to follow a 'sexual flow' – a connection to the erotic.

For others, creating is channelled without conscious inspiration, without a preconceived idea of the outcome – an image or form is not 'received' which needs to be brought into the earthly realm. Like the above participant, this way of creating involves surrender, but it is an automatic process of abstraction which has its own autonomy and action, with no preconceived outcome. There are no rules. The ecstasy and lovemaking with the Divine, the other, is through the joy of the journey. The process itself is sacred, not the outcome. This woman's experience of 'fluid art' was relational, full of love and a two-way interaction with something 'other' than Self. As in human-to-human love making, there is a push and pull, giving and receiving, doing and surrender, wildness, and gentleness. Her description of her creating process was erotic, sensual, and ecstatic but also deeply reverent. It was akin to the intimacy of co-creating with a Lover, who is in this case, the Divine.

She explained, 'I started with acrylics and the pouring method of thinning out the medium and letting things land where they wanted. I loved it, the swirls of colour, the mess that was created, the joy of the process. But I needed something more fluid. More wild and sensual, more untamed. I found alcohol inks, and instantly fell in love. The vibrancy of the colours, so rich, so intense. I realize I was trying to unleash myself in these works of abstraction. And in turn I wanted those who saw these pieces to take from it what they saw, not what I told them to see. I cannot control these colours and that is the beauty of it. It is sheer abandon, like the throes of ecstasy, dancing, merging, flowing, being. I may move them along, but they decide what they want to be. I was able to deeply connect with my own sensual nature through this art form. It is an act of beautiful surrender. Relinquishing control, and letting things be. Appreciating the process, enjoying the moment'.

Through the process she both gives herself fully and owns and knows herself fully. As Audre Lorde writes in *Uses of the Erotic: The Erotic as Power*, 'the erotic is a measure between the beginnings of our sense of self and the chaos of our strongest feelings. It is an internal sense of satisfaction to which, once we have experienced it, we know we can aspire'. It is a beautiful sacred Divine paradox. Lifeforce and the Divine inhabit the colours and art materials themselves. There is no distinction between divinity and matter. Another woman spoke similarly saying that her experience of creating is 'tantric' and a journey of 'embodying oneness'.

In addition to creating through art, this participant is also a writer. However, she described that there is an erotic energy, a full-bodied aliveness of the supernatural, the sacred, in art which cannot be felt or experienced through words. She explained, 'I am a firm believer that life is meant to be lived in full colour. As a writer, I realized that words can only go so far, and that visual art has its own magic and power'.

Another participant described how during times when she is not in a relationship she does not engage in sexual activity and therefore her sexual energy is channelled into creative projects. She described a process of sublimation of the erotic, her lifeforce into creating. Energy cannot be created or destroyed, only transformed. We are born with this energy and the ability to keep channelling it, through lovemaking with the Divine, into creating. Audre Lorde writes about how the erotic is far beyond 'just' sexual arousal: 'We tend to think of the erotic as an easy, tantalizing sexual arousal. I speak of the erotic as the deepest life force, a force which moves us toward living in a fundamental way'. For centuries celibate monks and nuns have been reporting that they practice sublimation of their sexual energy and urges away from sexual intimacy and pleasure, towards instead, charity work and creating 'with purpose'. Sexual energy and passion, it seems, can be transmuted into creativity – through a process of alchemy. Co-creating and birthing with the Divine moves from gestating and giving life to a human to gestating and giving life to a piece of art, book, sculpture, crafted piece, cake and so on. This is not to say that sexual energy cannot coexist and be channelled to create. Another participant explained how she consciously preserves and uses orgasm lifeforce and erotic energy in sacred creative processes to write poetry and song.

Several women expressed how crafting, especially textiles art, weaving and knitting was a sacred process through which they both commune and weave love with the Divine. There is an old saying, 'begin to weave and the divine will provide the thread'. Certainly, the therapeutic impact of moving mindfully into flow while weaving and knitting is undeniable and many women who offered their experiences to this book described how in this process and force, life itself, the Divine, flows through them and into the weave.

For me personally, creating happens with bigger objects. I make a display, some might call an altar, of items according to how I feel the Divine wants to express through me, visually, in a constructed form. Sometimes I may be out on a walk and my eye is drawn to an object – a leaf, stick or stone. I will bring it home as I know this will go on the table display – expressing the sacred in this earthly realm. Other times I might be in a charity shop and see an item, often incredibly old, which is symbolically holding a Divine message.

I then have a table where I create a devotional display according to festivals or seasons. I am fluidly guided erotically through instinct and intuition as I create a sacred representation of my relationship with the other, the Divine.

Also, I ritually create, often spontaneously on the earth or on the floor in my house. I use candles, crystals, and natural objects to creatively express my prayer or intention in an automatic and fluid way. I do not plan what I make. I have items and then allow eros and the divine to express through the objects. This is not a conscious process – it is prayerful and a flow.

Sometimes I will grab 'ordinary' household objects, such as a cup from the kitchen, if I feel they can represent metaphorically and symbolically what needs to be there. Ordinary and mundane objects take a sacred role in a story or picture which is organically built in a two-way relationship between me and the Divine. I like to sit on the floor and move, so that the creating is a fully embodied process.

Try this: Creating fluidly and with your whole body

This month, the intention is for you to experiment with creating fluidly and without an objective or expected outcome. You allow yourself to be moved. You can do this in whatever way you would like, and ideally, you will do this in at least two contrasting ways, a couple of weeks apart.

Here are two suggestions:

1. **ART**

   Get a big piece of paper, ideally A1 size and choose your art medium. The best medium to use for this sort of activity is paint, pastels, or big crayons.

   Choose a time and space for the activity where you will not be disturbed for 30–60 minutes.

   Put down newspaper or sheets to protect the surface on which you are working.

   Take a moment to drop into your body. Stand up. Breathe. Feel your feet on the ground. Orient to the space. Look from left to right, then floor to ceiling. Place one hand on your sacral/womb space and one hand on your heart. Connect and breathe.

   Try and stay standing up for the activity.

   If you are using paint and can put your hands in it, then do. If not, pick up a pastel/crayon – one in each hand.

   Take a moment to connect to the paint, pastel, or crayon. Feel the texture, look at the colour, connect to the smell.

   Then connect with the paper. Make big or small strokes across the page. Lean your whole body into it. Move your body as you create and draw.

   Keep going with this process – just allow. Change colours of the paint, pastel, crayon or do not. Allow the creating to unfold and flow without expectation.

   When it all feels complete step away. Tidy up.

   Leave what you have created to dry and settle, and for the following week look at it daily. Notice your feelings, thoughts, body sensations. Notice what you interpret from it – what did you learn? Receive? Give?

   Reflect on how life, eros, the divine moved through you in the process.

2. DISPLAY

Choose a windowsill or small table for your display.

Go out for a walk and collect some natural objects you are drawn to.

Choose a time and space for the activity where you will not be disturbed for 30 minutes.

Clean the windowsill or small table.

Walk around the house and gather any objects to which you are drawn. They can be anything – ornaments, jewellery, photos, anything.

Take a moment to drop into your body. Stand up. Breathe. Feel your feet on the ground. Orient to the space. Look from left to right, then floor to ceiling. Place one hand on your sacral/womb space and one hand on your heart. Connect and breathe.

Try and stay standing up for the activity.

Then connect with the natural objects and objects from your house. Feel, see, and know how they want to be arranged. Take your time, move them if necessary. Allow the creating to unfold and flow without expectation.

When it all feels complete, step away. Tidy up.

Leave your display in place for the following week and look at it daily. Notice your feelings, thoughts, body sensations. Notice what you interpret from it – what did you learn? Receive? Give? What does it represent? What is it expressing?

Reflect on how life, eros, the divine moved through you in the process.

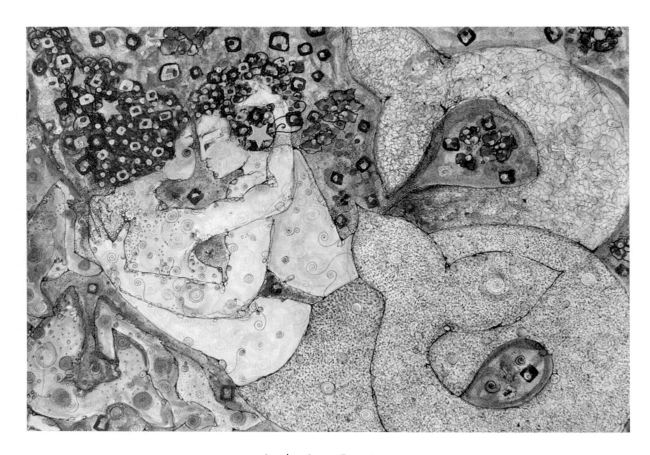

Art by Arna Baartz

Month 8

Theme: Relating

'We are born in relation, we live in relation, we die in relation'.
–Carter Heyward

'I define connection as the energy that exists between people when they feel seen, heard, and valued; when they can give and receive without judgment; and when they derive sustenance and strength from the relationship'.
–Brené Brown

Discussion:

Maslow's hierarchy of needs states that once our basic physiological survival needs are met the needs for security, safety, love and belonging present themselves for fulfilment. Humans need humans. Humans need to relate – and through this relating, this friendship, intimacy, affection, love trust and acceptance, the Divine can be experienced and related with. 'I unite and create with the Divine', said one woman, 'through my need to connect'.

Whether introverted or extroverted, interpersonal relating is necessary for aliveness and sustaining our life. One woman described the erotic as the 'experience of true connection – an understanding of one another and sharing'. We need community to be well and flourish. Sonya Renee-Taylor writes in her book, The *Body is Not an Apology: The Power of Radical Self-Love* about 'community as cure' – in that it offers collective compassion and a space to be vulnerable and share secrets. Community is miraculous. Many respondents to this book talked about the sacredness of 'sisterhood' – the sustenance and spirituality of it; the Divine dimension of it. The ecstasy, the comfort, the energy of aliveness it generates. The connectivity it gifts. 'I feel most alive with women in ceremony' said one participant. Another expressed, 'gathering with women in a circle or creating ceremony – I feel it – a presence so vast that it consumes me'.

Brené Brown talks and writes a lot about shame (which can result from sacred wounding), and she emphasises discernment when choosing those to hold space for and to listen to our deepest pain, whilst also celebrating our successes. She explains 'our stories are not meant for everyone. Hearing them is a privilege and we should always ask ourselves this before we share: Who has earned the right to hear my story? If we have one or two people in our lives who can sit with us and hold space for our shame stories, and love us for our strengths and struggles, we are incredibly lucky'. These relationships have an 'extra-ordinary' dimension – a sacred aspect – a spiritual and Divine essence. There is a sacred safety in these interactions, as if the life moment is held by the Divine. As one participant expressed, the Divine flows 'when I am being met in full bodied presence and able to share my little mundane and vulnerable truths'.

The participant whose experiences I described in an earlier chapter described a transcendent and extra-ordinary moment in relating in a different way. She described it as if this synchronicity, this blissful and ecstatic moment had been Divinely orchestrated and gifted. There was a numinous quality of the out of character behaviour of her partner which resulted in a Divinely erotic and deep moment of relating. We were both moved to tears as she recalled the memory. She talked about her love of 'cheesy musicals', those with a hero/heroine narrative, 'an invitation to the masculine and feminine to dance'. One of her favourites was *West Side Story*. She explained that what happened in the relating between her and her partner in the event she went on to describe was atypical – not the norm. She recalled 'I was in the bathroom and he's outside. The song, 'There's a time for us' from West Side Story came on the radio. My partner came to the bathroom with his hand out and we danced. This is an archetypical moment. The masculine says, 'come dance with me' and we dance, and it is ecstatic, erotic, and beautiful. The two become one. Something is channelled through us. It is simple and yet so profound'.

Relationships, it seems, are a spiritual experience, an interaction, learning and growth space for soul, some suggest. The sacredness of having someone hold space for our vulnerabilities can feel like being held by the Divine – that all layers of pretence and falsity are no longer needed, and we are liberated, free to be in our erotic innocence – full of lifeforce and aliveness. One participant described this as a playful, uninhibited experience – ecstatically joyful. She expressed that 'aliveness for me comes into play through true connection. Connection with others, connection with nature. It is when I feel synced with a being (human, river, woods) and fully present in the moment. It is when I experience a level of joy so high that I forget about expressing my emotions within societal norms. The mask slips away and I am free to be me – isn't that a joy in itself?!' Another participant described how she felt some relating is predestined and contracted by Soul for this lifetime so that love can be made and sacred pacts fulfilled. These encounters are Divinely ordained. On meeting her partner, she felt as if she was 'reconnecting with my best friend'. She also intuitively received the message 'your lover has been returned to you' and that they were choosing each other again and will always.

Shared connection was a theme for participants when they felt most connected with the Divine. A sharing of creative group experience was when lovemaking with the Divine occurred for one woman who said she felt the Divine and Life uniting within her when 'rehearsing, acting, singing and being with fellow creatives'. There were also contrasting expressions of relating in which Divine lovemaking and weaving occurs for other women. One participant expressed that this is felt in conversations which are 'deep, spiritual and participatory' and have a seriousness to them, whilst other women explained that playfulness, lightness, and laughter in relating were erotic and sacred – and within this they feel fully alive, and love is made with the Divine. One participant expressed this as 'when I am playing and joking, and being kind of edgy, pushing limits as a sacred trickster'. Grounding the Divine into day-to-day life allows all aspects of relating to be sacred. Rev Rowan Bombadil writes in *Igniting Intimacy* that the Divine is 'more akin to an annoying best friend'.

Love is made in relating when we see and greet the Divine in the other respectfully and reverently. This allows us to share commonality, see the goodness through the wounding and cultivate shared compassion. Relating then takes on a transcendent aspect, similar to the Hindu concept of 'namaste' – a recognition of the sameness and oneness of the Divine in yourself and the other and a reverent and sacred honouring of this. One participant expressed that with her partner she creates 'a field of love' and moves from the head to the heart 'allowing the heart to open to them and the universe (Divine)'.

One of the most prominent writers on the divinity of relating is the philosopher, Martin Buber. He wrote about the I-Thou in relating. He explained that in communicating with the Thou, the other, we are communicating with the Divine and this gives relating and therefore life, meaning. Relating as I-Thou is sacred – love is the subject of the relating, as is the experience of unity and a direct relationship with the Divine. There are no rules or obstructions.

In *Urban Tantra,* Barbara Carrellas describes an I-Thou experience of relating, a total sense of oneness and unity, during a paid lap dancing session. There are no words just the usual routine, during which the Divine is ecstatically, mystically, and erotically encountered. She writes, 'We are part of all that we can perceive and simultaneously at the centre of it all. We know everything about each other and know each other forever in that moment'. The I-Thou, unity with The Divine in relating, is not bound by morality, ethics, behaviour expectations, rules, dogma, doctrine, and religious commands. It is an encounter.

One participant shared at length about her experience of polyamory and that practising this way of relating has taught her 'we are all love, all part of the Divine'. She also considers it 'inseparable' from her 'spiritual evolution' and is her 'spiritual path' and 'an evolutionary journey of moving ever closer to pure love. Relating this way has brought her 'closer to my spiritual self'. She explained that 'pure love' in relating 'can never be wrong' and that this is 'the essential driver of my life'. 'I've always loved more than one person intensely – even if it had not been expressed sexually' she said. Her experience of relating through polyamory centralises a lovemaking with the Divine within love and a unifying and unity through this alongside spiritual evolution. Ecstasy is within the love expressed and created within and through multi-relating. Polyamory is her aliveness, her erotic charge, as in her lifeforce and a deeply sacred practice.

Here is her longer share about this practice:

> 'When I first came across the term polyamory – it was an epiphany – the curtains had been drawn for the first time in my life. I knew that was the essential core identity of who I am. It is not a lifestyle choice for me – it is for some people who practise polyamory or open relationships – but for me it is who I always know I have been. Through the practise of polyamory, I have shed cultural stories about myself and my relationships that I had unthinkingly swallowed. They no longer serve me. I have experienced the wonderful emotion of compersion – if someone I love also loves another that can be a source of joy and happiness. In developing my capacity for loving multiple persons, I have felt the release of ego, a giving of mutual freedom and trust where love is the central force. Polyamory challenges a sense of control and ownership; this has led to more of an ability to express and view the world with love. It has brought into focus my relationships as living, growing, expanding processes, not static statuses. To be in multiple relationships requires huge amounts of communication and compassion. It has brought a radical honesty in to my life and prioritised the care and love for others, and indeed myself'.

My own personal experience of the sacredness, ecstasy, and erotic nature of Divine union through relating has occurred in moments of heartbreak and vulnerability. The times when I have truly allowed myself to be seen in deep distress and when I was met with full compassion are the moments that I have never felt more certain of the presence of the Divine in the world. To be truly witnessed is elating, ecstatic in the relief and comfort it provides. To have space held whilst I cry and breakdown feels like a sacred container guarded and held by a Divine presence.

Equally, the times I have worked therapeutically with other women and have heard their stories of pain and grief, joy, and pleasure, I feel and see the Divine within them and greet all they bring with Divine presence within me – heart to heart – open and yet held in an energy of pure nonjudgement and love which is beyond either of us. I am Divine – they are Divine – the 'we' is Divine – all held within Divine presence. It is mystical and beyond rational description or explanation.

Colouring Sheet by Kat Shaw – from *I Am a Goddess: Colour Your Way to Self-Love*

Try this: Divine relating. Seeing the Divine in self and in other

Part 1: Seeing the Divine in Self.

Do this practice every day for two weeks.

Set aside 10-15 minutes at the same time each day.

Find a room with a mirror where you will be undisturbed.

Ground yourself at the start of the practise. Feel your feet on the floor. Look around the room – floor to ceiling, left to right. Take a conscious breath.

Place your hand on your heart.

Look into the mirror. Pause. Feel and notice what it is like to consciously look into your own eyes.

Take your time. Allow any emotions to arise. You are divinely relating with yourself.

Look again into your eyes and set the intention to see your own divinity.

See yourself as Divine. Give your Divine Self presence.

Keep connected to your heart – place your hand on your heart.

Ask your Divinity to speak with you or message you. You may speak aloud, or you may feel or just know what your Divine self wants to express or wants you to know. Be open to receive.

When the practice feels complete jot down anything you want to remember and write down how it felt to do the practice that day.

Reflect on the two-week experience.

Part 2: Seeing the Divine in Other (this can be a person, a tree or plant, or animal).

Do this practice every day for two weeks.

Set aside 10-15 minutes each day.

Choose the 'other' you want to Divinely relate to. This could be another person, or a tree/plant or a pet, for example. If it is with a person you may want to explain what you are doing.

Ground yourself at the start of the practise. Feel your feet on the floor. Look around the room – floor to ceiling, left to right. Take a conscious breath.

Place your hand on your heart.

Look at the person. Pause. Feel and notice what it is like to consciously look into their eyes. OR stroke or hold the pet or touch the tree. Pause, feel, and notice what it is like to connect.

Take your time. Allow any emotions to arise. You are divinely relating with the Divine of the other.

Look again into their eyes, or stroke the pet, touch the tree, and set the intention to see or feel their own divinity.

Then connect to yourself as Divine. Give your Divine presence to the other.

Keep connected to your heart by placing your hand on your heart.

Ask to receive from the Divinity of the other in some way. You may feel or just know what they are Divinely expressing or want you to know. Be open to receive.

When the practice feels complete, jot down anything you want to remember and write down how it felt to do the practice that day.

Reflect on the two-week experience.

Art by Arna Baartz

'Paradise is attained by touch'.
–Helen Keller

'Of all the gifts we can give to people, the gift of our touch is one of the most priceless. Through our hands we convey a kind of radiance. A warmth seeps out from our inner fire, a wrap for someone's chill, a light for another's dark'.
–Jan Phillips

Discussion:

Without touch, humans experience increased nervous system activation – stress and anxiety, alongside risk to overall health and wellbeing, physical and mental – and lack of touch can lead to depression and social disconnection. Skin-to-skin contact stimulates oxytocin (the love and connection hormone), serotonin (the mood boosting chemical) and dopamine (the pleasure neurotransmitter). In this animalistic need we see love is inseparable from our feral aspect and that the animal part of us is sacred in its desire to give and receive kindness.

Like all mammals, we are hard-wired to be affectionately and tenderly touched throughout our entire lifespan and the sense of touch is one of the first senses we develop in utero. It is our first experience of touch, connectivity and sacred relating to other. The sacredness of pregnancy –sharing of our body with another, body-to-body touching, for nine months – was shared as a miraculous process by several of the participants. Participants described experiencing pregnancy as 'a divine mission' and a 'cocreation with the Divine and Soul of the baby'. There was a numinous aspect to gestation and a spiritual dimension. One woman described it as 'soul touching soul, heart touching heart, human and the Divine creating love incarnate'.

Participants shared the erotic power of the birthing process too. During labour, some women described moving into 'sacred time' and a 'sacred space'. Ordinary time was suspended, and time and space enter a mystical dimension. Some felt the presence of the Divine enveloping them. Some expressed that they themselves became the Divine when labour quickened. There was a sense of uniting with the Divine to bring the child through the birth canal – the touch of each contraction 'powered by an erotic lifeforce greater than that of human origin' – making love with the Divine to 'birth love, through erotic love' and the power of the touch of the mother's body ecstatically giving birth and life to the baby. One participant explained that she could not have birthed just as 'herself' and 'on her own' – she didn't have the capacity to deal with the pain or she felt 'the power to get through the pushing stage' and so it was through 'activating the Divine within her' and uniting with the Divine power that she was able to get through the labour process. All participants who described birth as an erotic and sacred journey said the skin-to-skin contact of baby on their body, the first moment of touch when the baby was born, was 'pure ecstasy' and as one woman said, 'touching my baby for the first time strengthened my conviction that there is a Divine and it is the power of pure love'.

The touch of breastfeeding – baby's mouth at Mother's breast, receiving nourishment – was described as 'sacred' and 'ecstatic'. In this natural, day-to-day, mundane (and at times) tedious fully embodied act, women experienced a simultaneous deepening of their spirituality and womanhood. The eroticism of this was described as a 'deep satisfaction', not in a pornographic or sexual way, but a profound feeling of fulfilment and empowerment. One woman said that after giving birth and breastfeeding she 'finally felt, as well as knew, her own ability to create and sustain life from her own lifeforce and that she herself was the 'Divine' – it was inseparable from this creative ability. The instinctive ability of the baby to find the breast, latch on and receive the perfect sustenance for their holistic growth again was considered sacred. One participant describes the ecstatic bonding of the touch of child's mouth around the nipple and her hands on the breast as highly and innocently erotic – a 'divine uniting of pleasure and innocence, power and vulnerability'. There is no doubt that Divine love weaves through the feeding process and that the 'soul as well as the body is fed'.

Several participants talked about the sacred and ecstatic experience of a hug. That a hug can activate the erotic flow, a full feeling of aliveness. As we embrace, we embrace the Divine in the other and we are the Divine for the other. We also step into sacred time. Hugs cannot be rushed, and they cultivate presence – Divine connection. It can feel heavenly to embrace a loved one or good friend after a long time apart and there can be a reconnection at a soul level through this. There is an amplification of erotic lifeforce and heart-to-heart meeting? One participant explained that even a 'brief touch and hug' can facilitate 'erotic and lifeforce connection', and indeed for her, so could a 'brief glance'. Similarly, 'holding hands one participant said, 'can send an electrical current of lifeforce, turn on a divine connection'. Another woman talked about the 'innocent erotic deliciousness of smelling and stroking the head of a new-born baby'. She described the touch as the 'Divine gifting love'.

Finally, several research contributors were massage therapists and body healers. Other women talked about the sacredness of having their nails done or haircut, through which they experienced positive touch. One participant said that when she offers reflexology, she 'feels it' (the Divine) flowing through her hands to the client. She also said that when she places her hands on the client's body, she can receive mystical visions, or she sees orbs. A massage therapist said that during massages she regularly receives 'sacred messages' from her clients – but she only passes them on if she feels the client won't 'think I'm weird'. Another massage therapist said that she feels that she 'mystically merges' with her clients as she works.

One participant, a tantric massage therapist, talked about the eroticism and sacredness of her practice. She explained that she takes 'more care, slows down and listens before she puts her hands on her client'. For her it's an 'honour to massage a body' and she 'honours every part' of her client, often, massaging according to 'her intuition'. She described one sacred experience when she massaged a woman who at the end 'cried a little and reached out to hug me. Thank you she said. I wasn't loved but I really felt loved during this massage'. This participant said that – from this experience she learned that 'eros and erotic energy is about love, not sex' and that it is 'non-hierarchical – who is the teacher and who is the student is not dependent on profession or age'. For her, the Divine is 'human' experience and human experience is Divine expression'. She said the 'human experience is sacredness'.

My own experience of mystical occurrences – when offering my clients energy medicine and hands-on somatic support – are numerous. I weave support and love into the client's body and nervous system through intention and touch, catalysing their inner healer and own lifeforce. I do this in relationship with life itself – the Divine – but also in relationship with sensation and the wisdom of the client's body which I listen to through touch. Touch is the most intimate and powerful supportive modality I am trained in – it is sacred. It is erotic in that I tune in and am guided by my own and my client's 'power which rises from our deepest and non-rational knowledge' and am calling on 'the lifeforce of women' which 'lies in a deeply… spiritual plane', *Uses of the Erotic: The Erotic as Power*, Audre Lorde. I know when the shift has taken place because I feel it. The ecstatic and Divine explosion of erotic within us 'is the power to inform and illuminate our actions upon the world around us', which causes us to 'begin to be responsible to ourselves in the deepest sense', Audre Lorde. We are empowered and ready to make the changes that our inner compass directs us towards. It is through touch – the mutual relating of my hand to my client's body that the Divine flow of eros activates this.

I am guided in this process through metaphorical mystical and symbolic remembrances as my unconscious story tells of the sacred rites and rituals of ancient priestesses. Touch deepens a soul-to-soul sacred dialogue which is non-verbal, and happens intuitively, telepathically, in another dimension. I open at a mystical level to the wisdom of the client and the love messages my own Divine self receives. Within the sacred space I see how touch was used to activate and weave love in ancient times. There is no distinction between my human and Divine self in these instances. The touch is a portal into sacred space and dimension and knowing.

Try this: Sacred affirming touch

*** Trauma-informed Practise ***

Touch for many can feel unsafe and challenging, especially if trauma has been experienced in this way. If this is the case for you, please adapt this month's practice to your capacity and comfort. Do not force your body to do anything that is uncomfortable. Feel free to omit the practice altogether if you prefer.

The practice this month is to have as many experiences as you can of positive touch and to reflect on the sacredness of it.

Try to experience as many of the experiences listed below as possible. You can ask trusted friends or family to engage in the practice with you if it feels right. It is a good idea to keep a journal and write a short paragraph about the experience for overall reflection at the end of the month. There are prompts below.

Suggested experiences:

- Hugs with family members
- Hugs with friends
- Hug with a pet
- Shake hands
- Hold hands
- Pat on the back
- Arm around the shoulder
- Cuddle a child
- Salsa or ballroom class (where there is pair dancing)
- Manicure or pedicure
- Hair cut
- Massage
- Reflexology
- Head massage

Journal prompts:

- What was it like to experience touch in this way?

- Did you experience a sacred aspect of the touch? If so, can you describe it?

- What was your experience of love through the touch you gave and received?

Spend time at the end of the month reflecting on all your experiences and what you have learnt.

Art by Arna Baartz

Month 10

Theme: Sexual Intimacy

'Transcendence, bliss, peace, transformation, healing. Yes, extraordinary sex can include feeling like you're melting into the universe and connecting with the divine in a way that changes you, heals you, and truly makes your life and relationships better'.

Magnificent sex 'takes them deeper into their personhood, even into their divinity, and takes them deeper into their partner's internal world'.
–Emily Nagoski, Come as you are: The surprising new science that will transform your sex life

Discussion:

Sexual intimacy is when two people consensually take part in sensual and sexual activity with one another. Touch is usually involved (but not always) and there is trust, vulnerability and open relating. Activities such as kissing, holding hands, touch, mutual self-pleasuring, other sexual acts, and sexual intercourse – or making love itself – are acts of sexual intimacy when there is mutual, authentic connection, honesty, closeness, and support. One woman explained that for her, 'touch, being able to hug, can be as ecstatic and erotic as sexual intercourse'.

In making love intimately with another, we make love with the Divine through relating (as was discussed in an earlier chapter) and then deepen the union with the Divine this way through the power and weaving of the sexual and intimate acts themselves. Relating is 'turbo charged' by the erotic current of the sexual and intimate act, which, according to Naomi Wolf, is biologically determined phenomena. She writes in her book *Vagina*, that 'the vagina and the mouth of the cervix seem to be evolutionarily rigged to need an 'other'.

In addition, sexual intimacy between a couple can activate ecstatic, blissful, and altered states of consciousness – cosmic, universal, or Divine consciousness and oneness or union. The moment of union resulting in these situations is a 'transfiguration' of human into Divine incarnated – a marrying of human and divine within flesh – and/or a 'transfiguration' of the human 'I/we' into cosmic and universal 'all' – and a marrying of the 'both/and'. As one participant explained, 'this brings to memory the Kiss: I loved a man a long time ago. He was beautiful. His kiss was the most exquisite kiss in the world. There was such meaning in his kiss. When I closed my eyes and we kissed, his kisses, our kisses, literally sent me into rapture, my whole body swooned like waves in the ocean and in my mind's eye, the most extraordinary thing of all. I saw galaxies, universes bursting with stars and light. I always knew that was a sacred gift. I treasure the memory. I have never known anything like it'.

There are so many ways the topic of sacred sexual intimacy can be approached and discussed. Ancient spiritual paths and writings do offer us something on this theme and demonstrate that sex and the Divine have coexisted harmoniously historically. Tantric sex and self-love are well-known practices of Hinduism and focus on meditative sexual activity for healing, intimacy, and transformation. Activation of kundalini or Shakti energy through sexual intimacy creates a sacred flow of eros, life force. One participant described that for her 'sexual energy starts at the root, from here it moves up and the heart opens', she then 'voices authentically' with her partner during intimacy and as they 'unite together, two becoming one, we move into ecstatic orgasm'. She explained that this is a sacred and Divine state but that it always begins with an earthy and earthly attraction and is always experienced through their physical human bodies.

The metaphor and symbol of the Hieros Gamos, or sacred marriage, was a ritual performed in ancient agricultural societies around the world – but most specifically in middle eastern countries and involved humans, re-enacting fertility rites and the holy marriage of God-Goddess, through procession, ceremony, gifts, purification, feast, and sexual intercourse. The purpose of it was to ensure a bountiful harvest, crop fertility and abundance so the community continued to thrive. Through sacred sexual union, the power of eros, lifeforce, flows for the good of all. One participant talked at length about her experience of this as a 'community priestess'. The sexual intimacy she shared with her partner did not involve touch as she had experienced serious sexual abuse from an early age and so was usually shared via telephone or texting. The sacredness of their relating in this way soon became apparent and she expressed how they were enacting and channelling what she called 'The Great Rite' – an aspect of the Hieros Gamos.

She explained about the Divine weaving through their sexual intimacy, which happened through intention and energetic realms rather than physical. She was noticeably certain that through the intimacy and erotic ecstasy she was sacredly serving the community and shapeshifting into the Divine, making love as deity. Here is her share: 'I was able to share sexual texting with C. We lived in different states at the time. I was able to feel his touch as he described what he was doing with me. I was able to respond and describe back to him what I was feeling and wanted him to feel that I was doing. Without touching myself, I orgasmed. I was floating in the ether, in his arms. He called me Goddess. I felt safe. We would continue to create ritual space together and celebrate the moon cycles and create magic – while in different states and via text or call. We would both feel the experience as though in person. There is a portion of a ritual called 'the Great Rite' – it is 'Symbolic Ritual Sex' where the Priest and Priestess invite a god and goddess to share their bodies. We found this happening for us. We have had shared dream experiences where in ritual, surrounded by community, we embodied deity. We enacted the great rite, then shared the loving, sexual energy release to heal our community'.

Sacredness and sexual intimacy are indistinguishable in some Indigenous cultures. Harmony of the earth, our body, cosmos, and sacred flow are one – so abundant pleasure and ecstasy created through sexual acts in human-to-human relationship benefits all aspects of the universe. Such is the law of Ayni, reciprocity, and balance. One woman expressed that 'sex and orgasm for me, at its best, dissolves the sense of separation between egos, separation of the physical, emotional, and spiritual realms. It connects me to all that is, the divine, the goddess, whatever you choose to call it, it reminds me, viscerally, that we are all love. I am aware of the connectedness of all living things, our interdependence'. Another participant described how she opens 'to her partner and the universe'. That, she said, 'is the key to making sex sacred'.

Shamanic sexual intimacy involves a channelling or connection to energies (some name as spirits) from other dimensions and accessed through altered states of consciousness during sexual intimate acts. Elders within Indigenous cultures mentored and tutored the initiated or selected leaders in these aspects of sex magic to activate a deeper flow of eros, fertility and prosperity of the society and the wisdom mind.

Spontaneous spiritual and Divine encounters and experiences can happen to the 'uninitiated and untutored' couple however, and through the research for this book I discovered are still happening today. One participant described her spiritual experience and union with the Divine through sexual intimacy with her partner. 'I have simultaneously experienced spiritual ecstasy during sex and orgasms with a lover. I realised afterwards I had always considered spiritual ecstasy to be something that was experienced alone. To experience it surrounding an orgasm with someone else gave it a deep resonance. It's always hard to describe such an ecstatic experience I think – and words never come close. It's entirely different from the physical and mental delight of orgasm, no matter how earth-shaking that is. My experience of spiritual ecstasy can only be described as transcending the ego, transcending the body and mind, experiencing the Oneness of the divine of absolute knowledge that we are energy, light and love. Words/art/music always seem pale imitations of the experience, but it remains a deep and revitalising well of joy for me'. Another woman shared how she has 'visons of a Temple experience' during sexual intimacy.

One participant described how she was experiencing blocks during sexual intimacy, and in exploring her sexuality and eroticism, she decided to 'now call in the Divine Feminine Goddess energy to help me to enjoy, receive and release' before sex. She was consciously choosing to cocreate ecstasy with the Divine. Another woman explained that she 'taps into the sacred sexual, the erotic, through physical connection with her partner. She was clear that she 'makes love with the Divine' during 'embodied and ecstatic union' with her partner. Quality is important over quantity during sexual intimacy, she further explained.

One share described the experience of making love with the Divine through sexual intimacy within her own marriage on numerous occasions. She explained 'I have felt and 'seen' a yin-yang merger of our collective energies shapeshifted into the symbol. During intercourse I felt and saw my whole self and energy curve and shift to the right and darken, whilst my husband's energy also curved and shifted to the left, clearing and lightening. Together we created the sphere and Divine union of wholeness. On another occasion during intercourse, I noticed an energy ball being generated between our sacral chakras. This was eros moving through the perineum and activating the sacral chakra in both of us. As we generated more and more sexual energy the sphere of eros moved out from our bodies and united to create one sphere which was deep inside of us and between us. This was a sacred, extraordinary, and ecstatic experience of making love with my husband and the Divine simultaneously. Finally, during one experience of sexual intimacy, immediately following our simultaneous orgasm, a blue light emanated from my womb. It felt blissful and I felt a shift, a clearing and opening in my womb space. My husband was extremely shocked, having not experienced anything like it before. The love making had been deeply reverently and sacred, as at the time, I was in therapy processing sexual trauma from a sexual assault which occurred at the age of fifteen. The 'purity' of our erotic connection, the sacredness and honouring of the intimacy and the vulnerability and deep trust of our relating, I believe, activated the divinity of sex, the healing potential which can occur in such circumstances. The healing which occurred at a womb level during that connection was profound and facilitated through the Divine weaving in our sexual act and a deepening of our bonding and love to a level deeper than either of us had thought possible'.

Art by Arna Baartz

Try this: Exploring the Hieros Gamos

*** Trauma-informed Practise ***

Sexual intimacy for many can feel unsafe and challenging, especially if trauma has been experienced in this way. If this is the case for you, please adapt this month's practise to your capacity and comfort. Do not force your body to do anything that is uncomfortable. Feel free to omit the practice altogether if you prefer.

I recognise that this is a potentially triggering or traumatising subject and exploration. I know this from first-hand experience due to the response I had to asking about it during research. As I explained earlier in the book, there was disgust, shock, embarrassment, shame, unease, activation, and anxiety. The reasons for this are a whole book in and of itself.

One participant expressed that we are taught to feel shame around the body and that 'the body is not *good* and that the mind is better'. Another woman explained erotic sexual intimacy and making love with the Divine this way 'is also a tough one for me as I shy away from this potential 'feeling' or emotion. Patriarchy and my religious upbringing are deeply embedded in my logical mind – however, I know that erotic does not necessarily have anything to do with sexual pleasure. I shy away from this word (and the feelings it arouses) but I also know I have very deep pent-up erotic energy somewhere in my lower belly'.

So please listen to yourself, your needs and capacity and honour them. You do not have to engage in any of the practices. If you do engage and it is too much, then stop.

It is only possible to participate in this practice if you are in an intimate relationship and you need to discuss the process with your partner and gain consent. My suggestion, if you are not, is to reflect and journal on experiences in previous intimate relationships if you have had one. Or, if you have not, or if you prefer, you could journal about what you imagine the sacredness of sexual intimacy may be.

The aim of the practice is to bring consciousness and meaning to your sexual intimacy. This means having a sacred intention whilst you are engaged in sexual intimacy – how you relate, touch, move. It is an exploration of the concept of your sexual intimate experiences with your partner being a ritual, a ceremony that serves a purpose, is a celebration or is supporting the manifestation of an outcome.

What to be curious about and what to explore this month:

- What is sexual intimacy like if you approach it as a sacred act?

- Can you feel the presence of the Divine during sexual intimacy?

- How does the erotic move through the sexual intimacy as lifeforce?

- What happens if before sexual intimacy begins you set the intention to unite with the Divine during it?

- If you and your partner approach the sexual intimacy as Divine beings what happens?
- How might sex and orgasm be Divine energy? What is its colour, consistency, sound, shape, purpose?

Ideas for a ritual to try for Sacred Sexual Intimacy:

- Spend some time with your partner speaking lovingly, sharing a meal which you both contribute to and prepare.
- Share a bath together before sexual intimacy begins.
- Light candles around the room.
- Agree on something you would both like to invite into your lives which will have a positive impact on both of you, your family and even your whole life. Examples include more peace, more space to connect and talk, planting a vegetable garden, volunteering together once a year.
- Hold that hope in your hearts and fill it with love as you connect with your partner. If you are able, embrace with your hands on each other's hearts for a time.
- Stay fully embodied and in the sensation, the lifeforce and the sacredness of your intimacy.
- Notice any experience of sacred ecstasy and Divine eroticism.

Throughout the month, reflect and journal. Notice any changes in your lives. Notice any changes in your relationship. Journal your thoughts on the following page.

Art by Arna Baartz

Month 11

Theme: Self Pleasure

'Your sexuality is the foundation of who you are – the low hum undercurrent of being alive'.
–Kimberly Ann Johnson

'Goddess of Sacred Sexuality

Awaken your Divine Feminine.

Awaken your Divine Masculine.

And allow the Sacred Marriage within to flow through your body.

Become enlivened in every cell.

Live in pure ecstasy.

Make love within every cell of your body.

Balanced, whole and in Divine Union'.

–Kat Shaw

Discussion:

In making love to ourselves, we make love to the Divine. Finding power in our own self touch is a reclamation of the erotic, of pure, innocent lifeforce. Consciously moving ourselves to orgasm is a sacred act through which we can ecstatically commune with the Divine.

The power of orgasm is far beyond the dictionary definition of 'intense or paroxysmal excitement especially' and 'the rapid pleasurable release of neuromuscular tensions at the height of sexual arousal that is usually accompanied by the ejaculation of semen in the male and by vaginal contractions in the female' (www.merriam-webster.com). I expect all of us who have experienced orgasm – especially through self-pleasure when we are able to build the experience and sensation at our own rate and in exactly the way which works for us – have asked is this really all they are?

One participant started the interview I had with her by telling the story of being in a yoga class where the group was discussing enlightenment – what it was like and how to achieve it. She told me she was perplexed at how 'in the head' the whole discussion was and that she declared to the group, 'Have you never had an orgasm?!' The participant clarified for me that I was not alone in making the connection between the ecstasy of orgasm – the otherworldliness the experience carries, Divine ecstasy, and accessing sacred dimensions.

Reclaiming sacredness alongside the power of orgasm is a radical and revolutionary act for women. It is an acknowledgement of the sacred Divine power which we generate, own and experience for our own erotic ecstasy. Personal experience is that orgasms – particularly through self-pleasure when held in a sacred energy, intention, and process – can be a portal into other dimensions, spaces, and timelines. They offer a doorway for us to walk through to expand our consciousness, our energy, our power. And they offer us the invitation of full divine and erotic embodiment.

One share explained that 'having had profound past life remembrances, of sacred Priestess initiations in many timelines and cultures, channelled 'Light' or Spirit and made intimate love with the Divine through self-pleasure, I know there is more than a physiological process going on! Physiologically, orgasm moves us into altered states of consciousness, and I have been a woman 'high on orgasm' which Naomi Wolf states in her book Vagina, allows us to 'go more deeply into a trance state than at any other time'.

It was curiosity about these experiences which prompted me to author this book as I felt there was a lot more to be said on this, far more than my voice alone could offer. What I became curious about, really curious about, was women's experiences – the collective – our contemporary, modern-day 'love-making' with the Divine in all its forms, moving eros through our body and the rapid, pleasurable release of divinity throughout the whole body via what we name as the physiological event of orgasm.

The Christian mystic St Teresa of Avila wrote of spiritual bliss in a deeply visceral way, akin to orgasm, in her autobiography, *The Life of Teresa of Jesus.* The passage below was the stimulus for Bernini's sculpture 'The Ecstasy', found in the Cornaro Chapel in the Italian church of Santa Maria Della Vittoria. She writes, 'I saw in his [the angel's] hand a long spear of gold, and at the iron's point there seemed to be a little fire. He appeared to me to be thrusting it at times into my heart, and to pierce my very entrails; when he drew it out, he seemed to draw them out also, and to leave me all on fire with a great love of God. The pain was so great, that it made me moan; and yet so surpassing was the sweetness of this excessive pain, that I could not wish to be rid of it'.

The way love making with the Divine has unfolded through self-pleasure practices for many is through intention, breath, and embodied journeying. Women have discovered how eros, lifeforce, can generate and pool at the perineum as self-pleasure begins. Breath can move the erotic energy through the body – focalising it in specific areas for greater expansion and inviting Divine healing there through this practice. As lifeforce starts to rise through the self-pleasuring, women can work with the breath to slow and restart and build it to orgasm. This is a sacred practice with the intention of filling up with Divine eros, Spirit, more lifeforce, with the intention of embodied ecstatic expansion to become more fully alive – human and divine. As Barbara Carrellas writes in *Urban Tantra: Sacred Sex for the Twenty-First Century*, 'what makes sex magic different from other types of magic or prayer is the sheer power of the erotic'.

Another way to sacredly work and experience self-pleasure, is by setting an intention to receive guidance during the practise, to manifest or to commune with the Divine. Ecstatic and divinely erotically charged shamanic journeys can result once the practice begins this way. One share expressed, 'I may get a clear sense of knowing what to do – an imaginative vision or felt sense. Sometimes I move into liminal realms and feel the presence of energies moving through me. I've experienced a penetrative sword of Light energy entering my solar plexus, the sensation of vaginal penetration of an energy crystal amplifying the lifeforce flow and fire blazing from my heart. In addition, I've moved through journeys with Light beings, the Christ, and ancient priestesses where I have received information of past life initiations or rites, I was part of and have also received energy 'upgrades' or clearing. All of this happens as the ecstatic energy builds to orgasm. It's pure magic'.

Rev Rowan Bombadil suggests that we invite 'the Divine into your masturbation adventures' and see what happens.

Shamanic journeying to and at the point of orgasm alone, i.e., not during intimate relating, was described by another woman but not during a self-pleasure practice – instead, it happened during a collective shamanic journey. This is a clear example of love making with the Divine through, initiated and led by the Divine within the sacred practice of shamanic journeying. The spiritual aspect of the experience is clearly evidence through her lack of words to describe it – it is a numinous event. Linking it to an earthly religious venue and occurrence, embodied the experience into human life, despite the meeting of spiritual beings. This is an erotic, sacred, ecstatic experience of union with the Divine within the human body, most, especially in the vulva. Here is her share – which I have imparted in full below:

'Somewhere right near the start of my experience with Shamanism I attended a day workshop and went on one of my first 'journeys'. It was an intense and somewhat life changing experience, one that at the time I barely had words for and certainly took me some time to understand the strong symbolism and experience of it all. When you enter a shamanic journey, you are awake and conscious but also aware of your deep connection to your inner self and consciousness – you're in a semi dream like state. I had started the journey imagining myself in a particular Temple I had visited in India, by the base of an ancient sacred tree, where, in real life, I had laid a garland of flowers. In the journey I seemed to stay at the base of the tree for some time until I placed a flower I had brought with me by the base of the tree. My consciousness went up through the tree and I journeyed in the Upper World, meeting a large black snake, a monk and a father and son – now I can't remember the details of all this part but at some point, I returned to the base of the tree where the flower was being worshipped. The beautiful flower in turn became my vulva, then returned back to the flower formation several times. I had a conscious sense that the flower was divine and a physical sensation at the same time of an orgasmic flow flooding through my body from the base chakra upwards. At this time, I knew very little about chakras at all, and I'd never heard of a full body orgasm, or an energetic orgasm.

The experience of this orgasm was so unexpected – I had never even heard of being able to orgasm without touch, with only the power of the mind, or even the breath, I couldn't really understand what was happening to me, but these intense ecstatic electric waves of pleasure and energy rushed through me, and I felt healed, whole, energised. I was connected to my deep intuitive self and knew that at that particular point in time my life was on the right track. I was loved and connected to the divine force of love. After the shamanic journey there was a time where we danced, and the waves of pure joy kept flooding through me. I felt its effects for days afterwards and the glow of the memory of this still feeds an internal well of joy and love.

This experience was really the start of a journey for me. It brought to life something I felt in theory but didn't practise in everyday life – that connection through our bodies to the divine, that we are beings of energy and light, that the best we can be is love and love is divine'.

In exploring our and other womens' bodies, the divinity of the vulva has been recognised. In looking at art, or photographs of their own vulva reflected back to them in a mirror, many women see a Goddess within the image. Many describe seeing the outline of Mother Mary in the vulva but at other times the energy of Kali appears from the shape, folds, and creases. Have you ever looked at your vulva? And if you have, what did you discover?

This is a share from a woman who, as part of the training she undertook to complete a certificate as a Somatic Erotic Educator, had to do a practice called vulva-gazing.

She explained, 'I had huge resistance to this. This wasn't because I'm closed down to the glory of my body or unable to celebrate and enjoy sexual pleasure, far from it! It was because I unconsciously knew that I would likely tap into a variety of trauma and that in doing so I'd get in touch with a power so strong that perhaps my nervous system wouldn't be able to handle it.

Thankfully, my teachers were trauma trained and aware of the potentiality and potency of the practice, so we were prepared and advised how to proceed in a trauma-informed way. Listen to the body. Take your time. Pause. Wait. Stop when you need it. In preparing for the practice, lighting candles, bathing, creating ritual and ceremony were suggested, and I told myself that this was something I needed to do to complete the course and I'd be fine. I began reverently, placing the mirror between my legs, and drew back the towel, pausing to integrate the sensations and emotions of apprehension. Then I looked – following the guidance to notice skin colour, shape and so on. I was taken aback by shock and a somatic response of disgust, so I paused again.

Integrated and processed, disgust rapidly transformed into utter rage. The fire of Goddess ignited within me and blazed through my mind. Anger at the conditioning of genital shame and abuse of women's vulvas – my vulva – physically and sexually was strongly felt. The patriarchal expectation around vulva aesthetic uniformity was what appalled me. I paused and felt the rage. I felt the presence of Kali in my vulva. She was strong – potent – lifegiving. I felt empowered.

And then swift sensations, emotions and thoughts of grace and beauty arrived. I softened. I looked again at the reflection and saw that Mother Mary had appeared. My vulva was – is –

Mother Goddess. The vagina is her body. The hooded clitoris is her cloaked head. The inner and outer labia, her arms and cloak around them. She was poised, open in unconditional love. It felt miraculous to see and feel my own Vulva Goddess and Divine Feminine embodiment.

As I rested into this revelation and looked again, I saw the almond eye of my vulva shapeshift again into a portal, a doorway, to another dimension. The portal to the womb cauldron and the dimension of Creatrix, Lover and Mother. Without Vulva Goddess, human life would cease to exist. Humankind's continuation depends on her yes. Without my consent man is no more. The power of that was phenomenal. As is the absolute certainty and knowing that it is Goddess that births God'.

One participant described at length how looking at her vulva is a sacred and spiritual self-pleasure practice for her and that she sees her vulva as the Divine. She called it a 'devotional practice', through which she connects with the Divine using self-pleasure and touch, alongside yoni gazing. For her 'connecting with the vulva is deeply spiritual and powerful'. She continued to explain that in connecting to her 'yoni' (the word she used for vulva), she connects to a 'gateway between realms and light' and to 'magnificence and my divinity'. 'In my pleasure I find my power' she said. Through self-touch, self-pleasure and yoni gazing she is 'no longer afraid, diminishing self' and is 'more powerful and braver' in her life. 'I fell in love with myself' by 'honouring my female body, which is magic' – Goddess.

She connects to Divinity through 'her yoni' by coming to it with 'acceptance'. 'It's radical', she said and 'things shift'. When she yoni gazes, she sees 'angels and Mary – Christian images which make me laugh but calm me on a deep level'. 'I access the Divine – feel love, a gentle loving presence. It is mystical and defies the practical mind. My yoni connects me to a deep place of healing – it's surprising. I also access memories and images of temples, places, priestessing – different realms which are very loving. I remember being with Isis and her priestesses and that I share their power. I realise how diminished we have become. Connecting to my yoni helps me answer questions from the place of soul – that part of me. It is magical, loving, powerful and healing. I have an experience of magic, a mystical and experiential event. Sometimes I experience rage – it creates a tidal wave of deep power at the soul and Divine layer. Mostly I have yoni bliss – it wants to be a mutual partner – worshipped and adored. It is a great loving partner. My sense of aliveness comes straight from my yoni. I have done a yoni gazing practice with another woman too during a worship. I knelt at her yoni and wept – as I realised, I was kneeling at the foot of Goddess'.

Self-described modern Priestesses are increasingly embracing the ancient path and medicine of Sacred Sexuality. The Hieros Gamos – re-enacting fertility rites and the holy marriage of God/Goddess discussed in the previous chapter – is a ritual many Priestesses and modern Witches are adopting within their sexual activities but also, from my own experience, within solo, sacred, self-pleasure practices.

One participant described an exercise she did with a sigil, alongside orgasmic energy, to manifest an intention, in order to graduate from the Temple of Witchcraft. This woman also shared her exploration with sex toys and self-pleasure to raise her kundalini, lifeforce and erotic sacred energy, which she awakens and invokes during the process. This is always done with clear intention, peace, abundance, and healing, for example – and alongside the invocation of Goddess.

She offered a detailed explanation of her sacred, erotic, and ecstatic practice of love making with the Divine in many forms of Goddess through invocation and kundalini energy. She described her 'sacred orgasms' which she experienced through 'snake-like movements' 'belly dancing', 'hip circles', 'song' and 'spinal undulations' and her feelings of Lilith within her – within her vulva – assisting the pleasure and the rising kundalini. Here is her longer share:

'After invoking Lilith in selflove the night before, I felt a presence looking out of my eyes. It felt peaceful and knowledgeable. I knew it was Lilith. This sensation emanating from my eyes has happened more than once. It was as if I were looking at the world from the eyes of a bird'. Could this be one reason that birds are often associated with the goddess? My third eye has been partially awakened, and I feel happier than ever. My guru, Anandi Ma said once the third eye is fully awakened one can be realized. It may take twenty years to do this. Anandi Ma uses her gaze in spiritual practices. She has even brought her guru Dhyan Yogi back to life just with her gaze!

I ask for eternal bliss and other intentions now after invoking goddesses in selflove making. I do this when I feel the kundalini shakti energy rise. It is felt during selflove making, as well as after climax. I have written poetry and songs in this state of kundalini awakening both during sex and after climax. I have also felt my neck spontaneously move like a snake, which is probably how the association of the snake was correlated to kundalini energy originally. Kundalini flows in lovemaking regardless of climax. In Ayurveda it is recommended to only have three orgasms per week, or one will lose ojas, or vital energy. I think each person or partnership should decide how many orgasms is too much by noticing their fatigue level.

I also ask Lilith, Ishtar, or Kali to move my body in any way they wish to raise my kundalini and climax. I often arch my back a little and tip my head back. This is like the fish yoga pose. I found that this opens my breathing and allows kundalini to rise through my throat chakra into my third eye. I sometimes use breath of fire to raise my kundalini. If I stimulate my clitoris and place one hand on the top of my head, kundalini rises but it gives me a headache afterwards. I figured out intuitively that I could complete an energy circuit by massaging my third eye or the inside of my belly button instead of holding my crown. This allowed the kundalini to move upward without being blocked at the crown. I offer some of the energy created to the Earth as an offering to my patron goddess Freyja and to the cosmos. Inanna and Ishtar were considered goddesses of both heaven and earth, so I want to honour the cosmos as well.

I try to hold on to the raised energy/kundalini shakti after orgasm. The energy that is raised is offered to my patron goddess, Freyja, and to the land itself. I ask for intentions when I experience the kundalini energy. Once I held onto the energy after getting out of bed in the morning and used the energy to write poetry with my kundalini raised. The poem turned out to be a song I wrote to Lilith and sang for the three days of the new moon. I felt very whole and satisfied spiritually that day.

This energy flow has created great joy in my life, and I am singing all the time. I feel abundant without any lack both physically and spiritually. I no longer have a sense of longing for anyone or anything outside myself, as I feel complete and satisfied very deep within my soul'.

She concluded by saying that regarding intentions – *whatever she asks for on behalf of others* she receives herself too.

Making love with the Divine moves self-pleasure into the realms of mysticism and opens up an erotic portal to past-life remembrances and re-embodiment of Sacred Feminine gnosis. Energetically we are offered the opportunity to expand, commune with cosmic energy and integrate and balance yin and yang – receiving and giving – feminine and masculine within us. We can connect to our own divinity, Goddess/God within us. Calling in (through the imaginal realms, eros, inspiration and the flow of Spirit), can support transcendent orgasm, energy, and consciousness expansion – and a deeper communion with the Sacred, within and without, above and below.

One participant offered me a written submission and stated, 'I wanted to start with self-pleasure'. She described her process:

'Taking my time to feel really comfortable, there must be peace around me and a bit of me time. My breathing becomes deeper, and I listen to my body, I sense the urgency which rises up in me and begins to take over all day-to-day thoughts as the focus becomes only about connecting. My body is urging me to vibrate and move and connect with ecstasy albeit brief, the intention and the drive is to both connect and release. I access a sensual plane, a place that is always there, a loving breathing space devoted to union and ecstasies. It vibrates with sexual electricity, and it is here that my orgasm – like an ecstatic energy, like a beautiful musical note – needs to explode and express itself as it simultaneously spreads out across the cosmos, across the plane, at one and mingling with all the stars. The connection and the release are all-encompassing and seem to cleanse my energies and reset my nervous system. It also is the most magical aid for me to fall asleep in a state of bliss'.

Art by Arna Baartz

Try this: Warming to the sacred spot

*** Trauma-informed Practise ***

Self-pleasure for many can feel unsafe and challenging, especially if sexual or religious trauma has been experienced. If this is the case for you, please adapt this month's practise to your capacity and comfort. Do not force your body to do anything which is uncomfortable. Feel free to omit the practice altogether if you prefer.

Like the last two months, this topic is extremely sensitive and triggering for many. And yet self-pleasure is a deeply sacred practice – honouring our bodies as Divine can be done through self-pleasure practices. Plus, as one participant said to me, 'Women need more orgasms and time for pleasure – I live both'. Orgasms themselves, however, are not the point of self-pleasuring practices. They may or may not happen. It's inconsequential. What is important is that we approach our body and begin to touch ourselves sacredly and remember the divinity of ourselves, our bodies and pleasure itself – uncoupling it from what we have been conditioned with and by – that the body is base and non-spiritual, and that pleasure is wasteful, 'sinful' and evil. Definitely time to undo this.

So, for this practice the goal is not self-pleasuring as in 'masturbation' or bringing yourself to orgasm – although that may be part of it if you want it to be. The intention of the practice is to experience approaching pleasure and the genital area as sacred and gently moving through the layers of discomfort, shame and disgust which may be associated with that area of the body. The intention is to allow you to 'warm' to your vulva via offering it warmth and comfort – bring lifeforce to the area, and in doing so, establish the Divine presence there.

For this practice you need:

- a warm bean bag or hot water bottle
- a candle
- matches

To begin, find a room where you will not be disturbed for 20-30 minutes. Take your time to orient to the space. Look around the room – left to right, 360 degrees, floor to ceiling.

- Find a place to sit – on a chair or the floor.

- Light the candle and set the intention to come into loving relationship with your body and pleasure.

- Place the bean bag or hot water bottle at the base of your torso – over the perineum and vulva.

- Take three deep breaths in and out of the vulva.

- Feel the sensation – the warmth, the grounding, the pleasure.

- Listen to your body.

- Wait. Allow any emotion to arise without judgement.

That may be enough for the two weeks – doing this daily – journaling about it.

For the next two weeks do the same practice but add in movement whilst you are sitting on the bean bag or hot water bottle – such as hip circles and rotations or pelvic rocks. Notice the sensation, pleasure, and feelings.

If you feel moved to touch or move in any other way, do – this is about self-pleasure and loving the divinity of the vulva and its lifeforce and sacred power.

Should you feel called to extend your practice you could try the vulva gazing practice described earlier in this chapter.

Journal about your experiences on the following pages.

Art by Kat Shaw

Month 12

Theme: Mysticism

'Meditating on the holiness of humanness is not unholy'.
– Mirabai Starr, *The Interior Castle. St Teresa of Avilla*

'There is passion burning in my soul,
Innate love trying to take flight,
Gliding, like a bird through the sky.
Dancing amongst the clouds.
Spirit blows a gentle breeze to help it on its way.
A perfect union.
This dance we do.
If we just let love lead the way'.
–Diane

Discussion:

This concluding chapter specifically addresses mysticism and the mystical experiences women shared during the research process – explicitly their intuitive knowing, their day-to-day direct union with the Divine and their accounts of what happened and how. This section will explore modern woman's experience of *mysticism* as defined in the following way:

1. the experience of mystical union or direct communion with ultimate reality reported by mystics

2. the belief that directs knowledge of God, spiritual truth, or ultimate reality can be attained through subjective experience (such as intuition or insight)

3. a theory postulating the possibility of direct and intuitive acquisition of ineffable knowledge or power

(www.merriam webster.com/dictionary/mysticism)

Interestingly, none of the participants named themselves as a mystic or as ever knowingly having had a mystical experience. This was not the language system they used. However, many women shared the importance of ritual, ceremony, meditation, and prayer – alongside intention, invocation and magic being key aspects of how they make love with the Divine. They revealed a mystical union they experienced from being intentionally sacred and honouring the Divine in these ways, whilst also evoking the power of the elements, elementals, and objects from nature.

Several women talked about the ecstatic and sacred energy generated from – and which weaves through and amongst – women in circle when they are creating ceremony with objects from nature, flowers, leaves, crystals. For example, making mandalas on the earth was a favoured practice, as was sitting in circle on the earth or outside around a fire – offering fallen leaves or sticks with gratitude into the centre – mystically connecting and communing with nature and elemental spirits. One participant talked about her knowledge of and connection with the Sheela na gig – carvings of naked women with overstated vulvas which stonemasons of old chiselled, possibly in honour of the 'Great Mother' – and how she connects with the mystical power of them through touching the stone. In earlier times it was thought that rubbing the relic brought fertility – an apparent lovemaking with the Divine through the portal of the vulva of Goddess.

From my own perspective I have experienced deeply mystical experiences whilst facilitating ancestral clearing work in circle, via cord cutting and ritual leaf blowing during a ceremony (a practice I was taught during my shamanic and energy medicine training). Collectively, invoking the power of benevolent ancestors and Dark Goddess creates a liminal and mystical space which allows for the convergence of several timelines and a repelling and removal of denser energies held within them. All the women I facilitated for in this space felt the presence of specific ancestors who offered generational dysfunction to them to be cord cut, dispelled, and healed. The divine energy mystically moved through the ceremony and created a new weave of love into the ancestral lineages of all present. This was done by the power of our collective life force and mystical intention.

One contributor talked about a solo practice, during which she moves and spirals her hips, 'using sacred words or chanting', to bring lifeforce energy up and through her entire energy system. Chanting she said moves her out of her 'mental space' and into mystical receptivity and direct communion with the Divine. Invocation of the Goddess Lilith or Shakti moves this erotic flow. With Goddess and intentionally raising kundalini she said she has been 'helped physically and emotionally' and through this 'intuitive process' she is ecstatically transformed. She receives direct and ineffable power. She lives in a 'happiness state' now because of this lovemaking with the Divine, with 'no feelings of lack'. A similar share from another woman described that in ritual she mystically becomes 'the chalice', which results in 'spontaneously banishing limitations and invoking joy and bliss' through which she celebrates 'the moon cycles and creates magic'. She was not taught this – it was a spontaneous and direct acquisition of knowing.

Another participant described in more detail how mystical union with the Divine is a nurturing and intimate process which empowers her. She explained that for her, lovemaking with the Divine is 'being 100% connected to the 'Source energy' where nothing material matters. It is spiritual connection, a feeling, sensing, communicating, asking, performing ceremony to honour myself and, Earth below and Heaven above. In ceremony with myself and The Divine, I use candles, smells, sound vibration, meditation, pull oracle cards and smudge). I sit quietly in the dark and listen, craft, and move my body gently. Sometimes I wake up early and just sit in silence – I love that –it makes me feel happy and grounded'.

Silence and solitude were recurrent themes and important parts of other women's shares. One woman explained, 'I make love with the Divine with full presence and conscious awareness, through ritual and ceremony. In solitude there is purity of love and I have found sacred union with the Divine'. It seems that within quiet it is easier to commune with the mystical self, the soul and hear guidance and the 'still small voice'. This is great advice. Mysticism, as Rev Rowan Bombadil states, is about opening up to 'let yourself be loved' and to 'breathe'.

Mystical union and the sacred are not the result of 'doing'. Making love with the Divine this way is about allowing and creating space for inner knowing and guidance to lead the way. A participant said that for her the sacred is 'not in productivity mode but instead is the love energy of the Divine. In holding the intention to make anything more of a prayer, connection, and conversation with the Divine, I have more presence'. In presence is spiritual truth and power. Another share stated, 'I personally have had a profound mystical experience whilst 'doing' nothing other than sitting in presence and asking to receive.

During my shamanic and energy medicine training I set the intention to open my heart. I waited. I focused on the intention. As I did so I felt the presence of the 'Christ' energy – not the being of Jesus – rather the sense of the power of Love. The energy was golden light but had a bodily shape. I continued to focus on the intention and felt the impulse to follow the Christ energy as it moved into and through my hand, up my arms and into my rib cage – deeply penetrating my body – and restarting my heart with a sudden blow. It felt like a defibrillator shock, and I jolted and felt intense pain in my chest – like it was stretching, expanding and a fire was moving through it. My theological lens could translate this as a baptism of the fire of the Holy Spirit. That language system does not adequately explain this mystical experience – which was overwhelming and entirely indescribable, and which set me on a path of lifechanging alignment with love'.

Major life events which impact us traumatically, alongside the stages of grief, are sacred spaces and holy ground in which the Divine can be present and through which we often connect to our Divinity for the first time. There is a mystical element to trauma – a paradoxical opening up to lifeforce, the erotic in the midst of paralysis and death. The weaving of the Divine within one participant's grief journey poignantly described this phenomena. She explained: 'I vividly remember the first time I knew that there was something much bigger than myself, guiding me. I was in the bath, and it was three days after losing my little boy. I was numb. That thirty minutes changed my direction and opened my mind to a whole new realisation. I'm not sure of the physics but I walked out of the bathroom a totally different woman – I know this wasn't from myself because I didn't have the strength or resolve to birth this new identity. I did know however, that a greater force had chosen at that moment to reveal its wonderment and magic with me. It was beyond my control'. Within death was life. The regenerative power of the erotic, her sacred spark, birthed a new beginning in the depths of darkness in despair.

In a way, not dissimilar to this, unexplained chronic pain can communicate the sacred desire for aliveness, a mystical knowing to be followed – the urging of the Divine longing to be embodied. For me pain is my erotic energy, my lifeforce, shouting for my attention. Pain mystically carries sacred information and messages. It is a way that my erotic desire to thrive and embody soul guides me towards love making and opportunities aligned with my Divine compass and drive. Pain guides me when I need to walk away or set boundaries – this ineffable knowledge and signalling is most clear during the times that the pain is strongest. Through listening to pain, I align and cocreate with the Divine.

Many women talked of love making with the Divine in a mystical and abstract way, using a variety of different words for erotic and lifeforce or kundalini – including Shakti, Chi, the flow of energy from a pure source and vitality. One woman described kundalini as the energy of the 'Goddess' in the spine. 'We raise energy in order to set our desire alight with it', Rev Rowan Bombadil writes, and from the research for this book it appears that this coupling with the energy supercharges mystical experiences.

During one interview the participant talked at length about this mystical energy. She said, 'we can't understand the extent of our power – it's limitless. I spontaneously asked the question one day, 'if I had no resistance, what would kundalini feel like?' It was blissful, every single part of me was relaxed and open. There was no distinction at all – everything was just one. I just need to drop my resistance to feel that'. For this woman, the Divine and lifeforce are one and the same with kundalini. It is the energy which keeps us alive, and it is through it we are Spirit – flesh and Spirit became one. She said she was 'tantric' and explained further that there is a 'sacred union where polarities come together at a zero-point, heart, and mind at zero point. Here there is a Divine explosion. We don't need to do anything to experience this – we are this power – we are where everything comes together as a point of power and lifeforce. We are not separate – we are the lifeforce – at an interdimensional, cellular level'. She went on to describe the importance of gratitude and appreciation of 'God, energy, oneness', which she said is 'genderless' and us. 'We are the God particle' she said, 'we can turn to it and remember and light up with it'. This 'sudden remembering that 'I am' – that's love making with the Divine. It opens the portal to wanting more'. Her process is to 'wake up and expand, growing sacred union, the oneness of Self' through 'mystical sexual realms, embodiment, movement, dance, music, art'.

The theme of extra-sensory perception and cosmic consciousness – enhanced colours, sounds, connection to the whole of existence ran through the shares I received, as did the idea of non-duality. Barbara Carrellas writes in *Urban Tantra* that at the heart of 'tantra' is the 'elimination of duality' and the view of 'the human body and earthly life as concrete manifestations of divine energy'. To banish or eliminate binary is to embrace tantric philosophy which takes us on a journey to wholeness and oneness. However, it is a transient experience as we are Divine but are also human and embodied – and within that we fuse the sacred and mundane. Some 'drink in' the sweetness there and then decide that they should stay in this state permanently. Take my advice: Let it go. It is neither good nor even possible to remain perpetually absorbed. Life is long and filled with strife', *The Interior Castle. St Teresa of Avilla. Translation and Introduction by Mirabai Starr*. As we know from the above share – within our human life and strife – we also make love, unite, and receive from the Divine. Trauma and our human pain have sacred aspects to them.

The mystery and mysticism of love was also an important theme in the shares of women. 'I am a love bubble' one participant said. Another concluded her interview saying that 'the Divine is love. It is where we come from and where we return when we drop this body. It is God Goddess, all that is. The sacred is anything that our hearts call us to. The ecstatic is the full somatic experience of dancing with the divine, whilst the erotic is pleasure, expansion, and an opening to receive and commune'. Similarly, one of the final shares I received towards the end of the research process was 'that we are beings of energy and light – the best we can be is love and love is divine'.

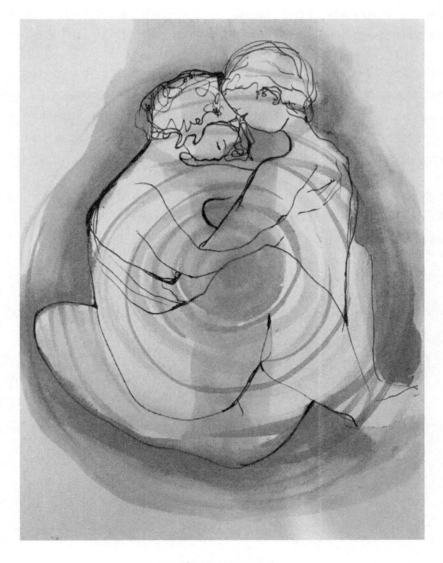

Art by Arna Baartz

Try this: Mystical knowing on our Human Life Journey

This final practice anchors us back into the sacredness of the messiness of our humanness and our mystical knowing, spiritual senses, and intuition within this.

For this practice you need:

- a notebook
- two different coloured pens
- a candle
- matches

Set aside 30-45 minutes twice a week for each of the four weeks of this month. This is eight sessions in total.

Set up the space where you will do the practice – a room where you will not be disturbed and are comfortable. Perhaps make a drink to have with you.

Light the candle and set the intention to connect to your mystical knowing, spiritual senses, and intuition. Choose one of the pens to answer the specified questions below. Tell yourself that when you pick up this pen and write in that colour, the answers and journaling will be led by your intuition – not your logical brain. Instruct the pen to do that. You can write the title/topic and the questions each time with the other coloured pen – this represents your logical mind.

During each session you will reflect on an aspect or age range of your life and journal to retrieve your mystical knowing from that time in your life. To facilitate this, each time you journal you will answer these five questions.

The Five Questions. Call on your intuition to answer them.

1. What am I pretending not to know about this aspect of my life/age range?

2. What does the Divine want me to remember about this aspect of my life/age range?

3. What have I forgotten about this aspect of my life/age range?

4. What do I know to be true about this aspect of my life/age range even though it can't be proven?

5. What magic was or is there and how was the Divine present in this aspect of my life/age range?

Aspect of life/age ranges to reflect upon in a session:

Session 1: Ages 1-7 years

Session 2: Parents

Session 3: Ages 7-12 years

Session 4: Friends

Session 5: Ages 13-18 years

Session 6: School

Session 7: Ages 18-28 years

Session 8: Body

An extension activity: Reflect on a time you experienced great challenge, difficulty, or trauma, and answer the five questions about that too.

Conclusion

Human and Divine – there is no separation. My hope it that this book has supported you to remember your tangible divinity. May the power of the erotic move through you as you now reclaim your full lifeforce and know that being alive is love making – a sacred and ecstatic experience of creation.

Kay Louise Aldred

Art by Kat Shaw

Further Exploration

Vagina. A New Biography – Naomi Wolf

The Interior Castle. St Teresa of Avilla – Translation and Introduction by Mirabai Starr

The Body is Not an Apology: The Power of Radical Self-Love –Sonya Renee-Taylor

Igniting Intimacy: Sex magic rituals for practical living and loving – Rev Rowan Bombadil

Urban Tantra: Sacred Sex for the Twenty-First Century – Barbara Carrellas

Ecstasy is Necessary: A Practical Guide – Barbara Carrellas

Dancing in the Flames, The Dark Goddess in the Transformation of Consciousness – Marion Woodman and Elinor Dickson

Arna Baartz: arnabaartz.com.au / facebook.com/ArnaBaartzArtist

Kat Shaw: katshaw.art / facebook.com/katshawartist

Making Love with the Divine Facebook Group:
facebook.com/groups/makinglovewiththedivine

Thank You

Thank you to all of **the women** who so graciously and generously shared their stories and experiences, their art and poetry. Without your voices and talents this book would not have been written.

Gratitude to **Trista Hendren**, Creatrix of Girl God Books, for your yes, your enthusiasm and support when I felt I could not go on with this book. A heartful thank you to **Anders** for creating the front cover and to **Pat Daly** for her thorough and careful editing and suggestions, which I deeply appreciate.

Huge appreciation to **Arna Baartz** for the powerful and exceptionally beautiful cover art and the stunning pieces throughout the book. Thanks also to **Kat Shaw** and **Katie Kavanagh** for offering their fabulous art to the book too.

And finally, as always, sacred thanks for my husband, **Dan**, for his tenderness, his sacred passion, and the generosity of his magnificent spirit.

**If you enjoyed this book, please consider writing a
brief review on Amazon and/or Goodreads.**

We LOVE photos of our readers with Girl God Books! Tag @girlgodbooks on social media – or
email them to support@girlgod.org.

What's Next?

A Poiesis of the Creative Cosmos: Celebrating Her within PaGaian Sacred Ceremony – Glenys Livingstone, Ph.D.

Somatic Shamanism: *Your Fleshy Knowing as the Tree of Life* – Kay Louise Aldred

Embodied Education: Creating Safe Space for Learning, Facilitating and Sharing – Kay Louise Aldred and Dan Aldred

Kali Rising: Holy Rage – Edited by C. Ara Campbell, Jaclyn Cherie, Trista Hendren, and Pat Daly

Women's Sovereignty and Body Autonomy Beyond Roe v. Wade – Edited by Trista Hendren, Arlene Bailey, Sharon Smith, and Pat Daly

Pain Perspectives: Finding Meaning in the Fire – Edited by Kay Louise Aldred, Trista Hendren, and Pat Daly

Goddess Chants and Songs Book – Edited by Trista Hendren, Anique Radiant Heart, and Pat Daly

Heart to Heart: Words from Goddess/Divine Feminine Wisdom – Kat Shaw

Imperfectly Fabulous – Kat Shaw

Out of Darkness She Speaks – Leonor Murciano-Luna, PhD

Anthologies and children's books on the Black Madonna, Mary Magdalene, Mother Mary, Cerridwen, Aradia, Kali, Brigid, Sophia, Spider Woman, Persephone, The Old Antlered One/Ancient Deer Goddess, An' Cailleach and Hecate are also in the works. Details to be announced.

http://thegirlgod.com/publishing.php

Printed in Great Britain
by Amazon

18340607R00072